Crewing Racing Dinghies and Keelboats

Bob Fisher

DODD, MEAD & COMPANY
NEW YORK

ISBN 0-396-07324-7
Library of Congress Catalog Card Number 75-39800
Printed in Great Britain

First published in Great Britain by
Stanford Maritime Ltd., 12 Long Acre,
London WC2E 9LP

For Carolyne and Alice

Contributing Authors

Peter Hunter—Prince of Wales International 14 Cup-winning crew.

Colin Turner—Twice Tempest World Champion crew.

Barry Dunning—Three times Merlin-Rocket National Champion crew.

Paul Davis—English National Flying Dutchman and World International Flying Dutchman Week-Champion crew. Also reserve Olympic trapeze crew.

Bob Bavier—Helmsman of America's Cup yacht *Constellation*

Adrian Jardine—5.5 metre Olympic Bronze Medal Crew, Mexico. National 12, Flying Dutchman and Flying 15 British National Champion on numerous occasions.

Graham M Hall—470 and Fireball U.S. National Champion

Judy Lawson—International 14 crew, one of America's top yachting writers.

Acknowledgements

Sometimes work is extremely pleasurable; preparing this book was one of those occasions. I wanted to provide crews and potential crews with some sort of guide for the job. A guide that would begin to tell the overall story, and would fill in most of the details; but also one which would stimulate crews to improve on their lot. Too many are taken for granted; some are sworn at for their ignorance; others for their incompetence, yet crewing in small boats can be rewarding. It is rewarding not only for what one can learn but also as a role in itself.

When I first started in the forward end of a racing dinghy almost everyone was in far greater ignorance of the sport than they are now. Those who were aware of what it was all about were doing all the winning and it was with a great deal of good fortune that I was able to crew for some of them. I realized then that there was much to learn and luckily I was picked by the patient ones. My fellow contributors to this book all admit similar fortunes. I hope that here is something that will help those who want to succeed as crews, a basis that will stand them in good stead should they not be lucky enough to find a patient skipper.

Therefore after thanking those who have helped directly with this book let me also acknowledge the cooperation of those who have helped indirectly, those skippers with whom I have sailed. Ron Norfolk, Jack Webb, Brian Walker, Dick Pitcher, John Partridge, Reg White, Richard Beales, Mike Patten, Terry Wade, Peter Schneidau, Phil Crawford, Jean Berger, Peter Bateman, Colin McKenzie, David Thomas, Paul Davies, Brian Saffery-Cooper, John Oakeley, Jack Knights and Simon Darney have unwittingly provided me with much of my material, by being at the back end of many of the boats that I have crewed. Ralph Rouse, Doug Whitehead, John Osborn, Richard Beales, Dick Lonton, Mike Fitzpatrick have similarly contributed by suffering the 'difficult end' whilst I drove. And all those crews who've been around the circuit who have discussed their problems, they too have helped.

Small boat sailing has been, and is, part of my way of life. Principally my view has been that of a crew; I wouldn't have wished it otherwise. I hope this book helps to make it more enjoyable for others.

Bob Fisher
1976.

Contents

Appendices

The whole philosophy of being a good crew is summed up in this picture. Gerry Mawson busily involved in the maintenance between races whilst skipper David Childs prepares himself mentally.

(John Hopwood)

1
The Reason Why

Crewing is just as specialized a department of small boat racing as being a skipper. There's as much to do, if not more, and it has just as significant an effect on the boat's performance. Yet for years it has been treated as a second class existence. Those days are rapidly passing with the increasing awareness by helmsmen of the role of their crews—the top helmsmen have been aware of this for years and that is why they are top.

Historically, the crew has had a rough deal. When yachts were the playthings of rich men and races were for purses of sovereigns or a substantial side bet, the crews were paid minions, subservient to a professional skipper whose word was law and whose pay was at least four times that of any of them. The owner came aboard to sit in a deck-chair and watch while his hirelings did their best to beat the hell out of one of his friends' boats. If they were successful a sovereign or two would be tossed into their midst to be shared out among them, and the owner would disappear for another week. Those days took a heavy knock from the Kaiser's War and were finally obliterated by Hitler's holocaust. However, the lord/serf relationship tended to persist, particularly in bigger boats. The owner-driver started to appear, followed by the amateur crew, but for many years a skipper's ability to get a crew depended on his ability to provide a first class yacht with food, drink and comfortable beds. Today, with the increase in crew availability the skipper depends on his ability afloat as his principal bait in attracting the best.

I personally prefer to crew. I think it's because I feel in

greater control of the situation in the front end, and I can contribute more to win races. I've had the joy of sailing with some extremely good helmsmen in a wide variety of boats, and from each of them I have gleaned a great deal of experience. It would be presumptuous to suggest that I was the first to make a scientific approach to crewing, but few have bothered to do much to develop their talents in this sphere until recently.

The three equal contributory factors in a successful racing boat are the helmsman, the crew and the boat. If any one of the three is substandard, the whole equipage will suffer. There is little the crew can do to improve the helmsman directly, but I hope to show that he can do a lot to enhance the skills of the man at the tiller. However, his own performance is in his own hands, and so is that of the boat, even before it goes in the water.

Most people go into crewing to learn—many from scratch. Certainly it's the best place to find out the truths about racing, and all helmsmen should spend an obligatory period crewing before they are allowed to steer a boat in a race. There's no faster way of finding how to get the best out of a boat than racing, and even if your eventual aim is to get your sailing kicks by cruising, a period of small boat racing is invaluable. Crews can progress from dinghies through day keelboats to ocean racers and will always be welcomed for their skills.

Crew's skill is rapidly becoming recognized at the prize tables. Not many classes have gone as far as the Flying Dutchman in having a World Championship trophy that splits equally between crew and helmsman, but they should. The Merlins and the Hornets have always recognized the crew's worth, and the Fireballs did from their inception. The added incentive gives a little more pleasure to crewing and it is equally deserved.

Crewing is not for the fame seekers, for hardly anyone has made a big name solely by crewing and in the Olympics it's difficult to find out who the crews are. There are notable exceptions—such as Keith Shackelton, Iain Macdonald-Smith and Barry Dunning—but even they have not made their fame on crewing alone. Yet the best crews are known to the top helmsman in every class, though their names may be far from household words. The satisfaction in crewing well is perhaps best realized by the invitation to crew for a top-class helmsman.

The sport of small boat sailing is developing so fast that the skill of crewing becomes greater each year. When Paul Elvstrom first treated the sport in the same way as any other athletic activity and trained for it, he was very much alone. It was considered 'not cricket' by the majority: now everyone who aims at major honours in small boat competition acknowledges the fact that physical fitness is important. The cavalier approach is fast dying out and the dedicated sailor is the successful sailor. Just how far you are prepared to dedicate yourself to the sport dictates the type of boat you will sail, and how successful you will be. The Olympic classes are for athletes, which is as it should be, and they are the ultimate level, but equally good sport can be obtained by crewing in another less demanding class as long as you are prepared to give your all to it. No matter what the boat, you will need to be fit to crew it properly. Stamina to sit out without pain through a race allows the brain to work better and to appreciate what's going on and the body to react faster. Because of the developments in the sport there is now more to think about while racing.

Perhaps the greatest value of a crew is as an ideas man. If something doesn't work properly the crew and skipper must find a way to make it work better, and beyond that, the crew must always be seeking to improve the gear in the boat to make his own job faster and easier. One classic example is the spinnaker halyard system used by John Caig and Jack Davis on *Jumping Jac*, their double World Champion Fireball. They appreciated the value of a quick hoist for the kite and decided to use a three-to-one whip at the top of the halyard. It meant that John had less than six feet of halyard to pull in the boat for the spinnaker to be fully up. This is the type of crew-oriented idea that helps to win races. Of course you cannot be expected to come up with one of these every day, but a constant review of the boat, the gear and its associated problems should be every crew's duty.

It is the crew's job to use his brain as well as his physique; he must be familiar with the racing rules and have a sound knowledge of tactics, only then can he contribute fully to the sailing of the boat in competition. The crew should be as well versed in the finer points of racing as the helmsman, as he is in a better position to assess the situation and control the tactical side of the race. But even if one reaches this sort of perfection, the good crew will still have the self-discipline to understand that the final decisions must be the skipper's.

Nevertheless, the crew must not be so subservient afloat that he never opens his mouth. Comments have value, but care must be taken in their timing. No helmsman wants a constant stream of chatter coming out of the front end of the boat, particularly while he rounds marks or is in close combat with a rival. What he does want to know is what's going on around, so that he doesn't have to look for himself and can concentrate on getting the boat through the water at the fastest possible speed. What will really put him off is a contradictory order without justification—that sort of thing should lead to the sack for the crew, anyway. A contradictory order must only come from the crew when to carry out the skipper's request will put the boat in danger. And always remember that what you want the skipper to hear is not for the ears of his rivals—so your voice level must be kept down. You can psyche your own helmsman into above-norm performance—remarks like 'You're killing them' as he is going well on the first beat might give him some encouragement to keep it up. I remember one race in the Australian National Hornet Championship when I kept up a stream of encouragements to Colin McKenzie at the back end. When we came ashore he admitted that unless he'd had me driving him on mentally he could have lost the urge and thereby the race and the Championship.

Ashore, crews must discuss the race with their helmsmen. Only in this way can both evaluate their performance as a team. Between them they must look objectively at their race and see where they went wrong—and even if they won there are still lessons to be learned. It may be that the minor chronic malaise of a fitting had contributed to a loss of places at a crucial point: this is when it should be discussed *and* something done about it—not afloat. A tactical error or a second class performance by anyone on board certainly needs reasoned discussion, and this should never be held in an acrimonious atmosphere. A row gets nobody anywhere. Analyze mistakes, and then try to prevent them happening again.

One attribute which all crews should possess is an irrepressible spirit. Coupled with a will to win this can be more use than almost anything else. When the chips are down and things look bleak there is one certain way for them to get worse: by acknowledging defeat. A good crew will make some uplifting suggestion, and it doesn't need to be far above trite as long as it is said in the right tone of voice to give his helmsman some encouragement. I can recall a race in the Soling Olympic trials at Poole when David Elphinstone and I were crewing for Terry Wade. We made a seconds error of judgment for our port tack start and then had to go under the sterns of the entire fleet. David looked back at Terry and with a chuckle said to me, 'That'll give him something to chase.' It may have had something to do with the fact that we were first at the weather mark.

Helmsmen should offer their crews the chance to steer as often as possible, and not just during the sail ashore when the race is over. By sailing the boat with the tiller in your hand, you best appreciate the helmsman's problems and how your actions can alleviate them. The effect that an over-sheeted spinnaker has on the helm as it makes the boat heel and creates drag around the rudder is just one of the things that a crew can only appreciate when it happens to him as he is steering. The top crew is the one who is as good, or almost as good, at the back end as the skipper: he needs to be.

A good crew doesn't need to be reminded to check over the boat before and after a race; he does it automatically. Everything needed must be in the boat before going afloat—it is more than embarrassing to be caught without a spinnaker boom. Tide times, sailing instructions and so on must be aboard.

Crews aren't bound by their pockets to which classes they sail, only by their ability. (They must, however, fully realize the limits of their ability if they are going to enjoy racing, and without enjoyment they should give it up.) Whatever you fancy is attainable; there are always crewing berths available to anyone who can fill them. The choice of keelboat or dinghy is yours, but do bear in mind that a six foot two inch fifteen stoner (210 pounds) is not much use in a twelve foot dinghy; neither is the seven stone weakling any good in a Tempest.

Get to know your skipper. Unless the two of you are compatible afloat and (less important) ashore, there is little hope of success. Success is the result of teamwork, and if you are prepared to devote yourself fully to the team you might consider joint ownership. This does ease the financial burden on the skipper and is bound to endear you to him. Since you are getting the fun out of it, it would seem a logical step. There are arguments for and against, but I am wholly for it.

Crewing is a collection of skills which are worth learning. There is a lot of satisfaction at the front end. Anyone getting depressed would do well to remember that yachting would be a poorer sport if there were only singlehanders.

In moments like this the crew would be better occupied sitting the boat upright and keeping the boom end away from the mark rather than staring fixedly at the buoy.

2
Shore Duties

Except for the hedonist, the pleasure derived from any leisure activity is directly proportional to the effort put in. This is even more true in competitive sport. There the measure of success determines the amount of enjoyment, and success is only forthcoming with effort. No cricketer would think of facing the bowling with a cracked bat, and neither should any competitive sailor think of entering a race with a boat which is not in peak winning condition. Getting and keeping the boat in prime shape is just as much a duty of the crew as of the helmsman. There is a lot of work to be done on a racing boat and it seems to take much less time when two people are working on them. Some are pretty unpleasant, dirty, wet jobs; others just fiddly and time consuming. Well done, all of them will have a direct effect on the boat's speed or the efficiency of the team. All, therefore, are worth doing.

Crews should start the season by helping with the annual fitting out. As sailing seasons have been extended and modern paints and varnishes have achieved greater durability, this arduous task no longer takes up most of the winter months. It has to be done, however, and if a fortnight of evenings and a couple of weekends have to be set aside, then it is the crew's duty to turn up and share the work.

Any good paint manufacturer's manual will tell you how to apply paint or varnish. Follow them and you won't go far wrong, but over many years I have learned one or two short cuts which can help alleviate the labour. On one job only there is no short cut and that's the rubbing down. Only hours of work can produce the right sort of surface on which to put the paint. Always start on the hull itself, because that is the part of the boat that's in the water and is the one from which there is the greatest return for hard work. If for any reason the fitting out gets cut short then at least the hull will have been done and the decks can be finished later. First of all, the boat must be thoroughly washed down with fresh water and detergent and then rinsed off with fresh water. This removes any salt, dirt and grease and some of the loose bits of paint. If it's a dinghy, turn it upside down and support it on trestles so that it is at the right height to work at. Too much stooping makes for backache and reduces efficiency after an hour or so. A keelboat must be well supported at the ends with most of the weight taken by the keel, otherwise the hull will distort badly while it is out of the water. Some of the smaller keelboats like the Star and Tempest take well to being laid on their sides for minor work, but they should not be left there long as their own weight on a small area of one side may permanently distort the hull.

The aim is to achieve a perfectly smooth surface over the whole hull. The existing surface is probably a mass of pits, scratches, dents and bare patches which must be built back up to the general surface layer before anything else can be done. First, loose material must be thoroughly cleaned away with coarse sandpaper and the whole lesion and surrounding area rubbed down. Then, in the case of bare patches, the priming coats must be built up and undercoat added. If, like me, you use one-coat polyurethane paint, the process is slightly quicker, but it must be stressed that though this patching up does take time, it is most important. Pits, scratches and the like should be filled in with a good stopping or filling compound. Don't expect to fill in deep marks in one go—the stopper shrinks slightly and leaves unsightly hollows. Not only that, as it shrinks it can pull away from the sides of the hollows and totally negate its purpose by falling out. When all the blemishes have been corrected the whole hull should be rubbed down with wet-and-dry paper until a smooth all-over finish is obtained.

If the grain shows through on a wooden hull the easiest way to counter the problem is by facing the hull with trowel cement. As purchased in a tin, this material is far too stiff to use; it must be thinned down on a mortar board with white spirit (turpentine) until it has the consistency of hot golden syrup. Then with a broad-bladed facing knife or wallpaper stripping knife it should be applied all over the hull *across* the grain of the wood. The cement is left in the hollows as the blade of the knife scrapes across the high spots of the grain. If the grain is bad the hull may need two coats of trowel cement before it is smooth enough to begin repainting. I find with a new hull that after a month or six weeks of sailing it pays to take it back into the shed and rub it down and face up with trowel cement, and then get a really good finish with another couple of coats of paint. It takes time for the paint to seep into the softer grain and seal the whole surface of the wood.

Fibreglass hulls present different problems. They still get bashed around in the same way, but painting is not one of their necessities. All deep blemishes should be partially filled with a resin mixture with a filler material added. Often this is nothing more than powdered french chalk. Then the whole scratch or pit must be finished with matching gel coat. Care must be taken not to use too much of this, as it will take an awful long time to rub back to the level of the rest of the surface. When it is back, some burnishing paste will finally smooth it in with the rest and this leaves a very fine surface. Don't be unduly perturbed if the new gel coat is a different shade of colour: it will blend in eventually.

While working on the hull it is as well to check the centreboard slot rubbers. I change mine about every six months as they are very vulnerable. New plastic strip is probably best if it can be made to fold around the leading and trailing edges of the centreboard. If too stiff it leaves a gap and this completely spoils its effect. The good crew will check the slot rubber before each race. A ruck in it or a bit dangling is going to have a major detrimental effect upon the boat's performance.

The protective metal or plastic strip along the midline of most wooden hulls and around the centreboard case should be carefully checked. It must be straight or it creates turbulence, and where two pieces meet the joint must be perfectly smooth. All the fastenings should be filed flush with the strip and the screwhead slots filled with stopper.

The anchorages for fittings which pierce the hull must be checked regularly. Self-bailers must be absolutely flush with the bottom of the boat; they cause enough drag when they are down, and there is no point in adding to this when they are up. Particular attention should be paid to the chainplate bolts to see that these are not pulling through the hull.

Once the exterior hull is perfect, the decks and interior can then receive their attention. I will grant that a boat with a grand piano finish does give its helmsman and crew a psychological advantage, but it is not essential. What is essential is a sound finish which keeps the water out. On older boats the likely bad spots are along the side of the centreboard case where it meets the hull, joints in the deck, around the heel of the mast, and the joint between the hull and the transom close by the hog. There is almost certainly bound to be loose and peeling varnish here and around the fittings.

There is no short cut to unbolting and unscrewing all the fittings. While they are off, a rewarding fireside job is to clean them all properly, removing corrosion and oiling all the working parts. The jaws of cam jam cleats should be examined and if they are badly worn, discarded. Where there is a little wear the jaws can be improved with a rat-tail file, particularly Tufnol and aluminium cams.

Varnish must be built up in the same way as the paint on the hull, using small amounts of matching filler and several coats of varnish in the hollows. Once the deck has been given a couple of complete coats and allowed to dry hard, it should be flattened off with 600 grade wet-and-dry abrasive paper. When this has been done it can be seen that water does not stay on the deck in droplets, but goes overboard quickly. Up to five pounds of water can be held on a Flying Dutchman because of this phenomenon, and since many hours have probably been spent in removing every surplus, and some not so surplus, it seems crazy not to get rid of this excess water.

Getting rid of weight in the boat is always a problem, unless one has a new boat with a few pounds of correctors in it to play with. Judicious chipping away of deck beams and lightening holes cut in knees and stringers can often get rid of a few pounds, but when such minor surgery is indulged in, care must be taken to seal all the newly exposed wood or water soaking in can easily outweigh the wood taken out. And I'll guarantee that there's at least one fitting on every boat which doesn't do anything—it has to come off and the screw holes have to be filled.

A check over the boat after racing will bring to light any imperfection and these should be rectified there and then. I remember that years ago Roy Bacon used to wander round his GP14 on a Sunday evening with a pot of varnish and a small camel hair brush and touch up all the scratches and knocks from the week. The boat looked as good as new four or five years after it was built.

The boat of any successful racing team is almost certainly immaculate. There is an awareness on the part of the good crew that he has a duty to make everything work properly, and to do this he puts in time. The helmsman, often shamed into it by the crew, puts in his fair share of work as well, and as there is no reason why the boat should deteriorate, it looks like new even though it isn't.

Centreboards, keels and rudders are the most significant potential drag producers in a racing boat. Any of these which are in bad shape must be discarded. A crew that knows how to make a good centreboard or rudder is worth his weight in gold. A basic knowledge of hydrodynamics is helpful, if only to appreciate what goes on around these foils; but practical wood-working ability is all-important.

When building a centreboard or rudder, the first choice to be made is the required section. Very accurate templates of the sections at regular intervals are then made. Choice of material is important: badly cured timber is bound to warp, and rarely is it possible to find a board that is big enough and stable enough. Quarter-sawn mahogany doesn't seem to exist these days, so a compromise is necessary which in many ways is better. Lengths of one and a half inch square mahogany already planed are laminated with resin glues into a board which will have better properties than the one-piece board. If the strips are turned alternately end for end, any twist that might develop in one is counteracted by the adjacent strip and a more stable board results. Sharp tools and a load of hard work will then produce the goods.

The choice of section is most important. Years ago the German small boat racing expert Dr Manfred Curry recommended the use of the Goetingen 444 section for both centreboards and rudder blades. Now the choice seems to be between the NACA 0006 and 0009 series of sections, with one major modification. The rear seven to eight per cent of the foil is cut off leaving a square trailing edge about one-tenth of an inch (2.5 mm) thick. This helps the water break away cleanly from the foil, but more importantly, it eliminates the need for a very thin piece of wood at the tail end which could vibrate, and make the rest of the board vibrate in sympathy. The energy consumed in producing this vibration detracts from the forward motion of the boat.

Once the centreboard or rudder has been shaped to fine limits in wood—and I am assured that it is possible with sharp tools to work to within three thousandths of an inch—it has to be finished with many thin coats of paint and light applications of trowel cement put on with a brush. White paint is the only surface finish that should be contemplated, and between each coat the paint should be rubbed down with wet-and-dry paper using a rubber sanding block.

Anything other than white paint can be a disaster. On one occasion I had a new Hornet which I rushed to finish on the day before a National Championship. In it I was going to use an old centreboard which had been stored in my garage for three years. To get a good finish on this board I quickly gave it a coat or two of Graphspeed and rubbed it down: it had a super finish in no time. However, it was a hot sunny day and I left the board out for a couple of hours in the sun while I worked on the boat. When I thought about putting it in, I found to my horror that it had warped badly. Full of cunning, I turned it over and left it in the sun for another couple of hours. It worked—the heat on the other side of the board counteracted the warp. With a sigh of relief I plunged the board into the sea (to temper it!) and quickly put it in the centreboard case before it could come to further harm. I must say that I was surprised that this board, which in its previous six years of life had shown no tendency to warp, had done so now, but I can only put it down to the totally non-reflective black graphite paint absorbing all the heat. The cure was as risky as it was effective, but it put a smile back into Philip Crawford's cheeks—he was at the helm that week.

Any chips, dents or scratches in a centreboard, rudder or keel must be dealt with immediately. The affected areas should be filled in, sanded down and refinished. Temporary repairs can be effected with fast-setting plastic putty, and the same material can be used to fair in iron keels.

Keels do have their own particular problems. In the main because they are iron and tend to weep rust. The permanent cure is to send the whole keel away for shot-blasting and galvanizing. This, is expensive, however, and in its place wire brushing, cold galvanizing, etching primer and many coats of paint are generally the answer. Any carelessness when loading a keelboat on a trailer is bound to result in further hard work, so the crew must stay around and make sure nothing goes wrong. Some boats have retracting keels for trailing, but if they are to be at the front of the fleet they will never retract their keels. All the top Tempests now firmly wedge their keels in the slot at the top and bottom and fill the slot around the bottom with cement so that a perfectly smooth finish is obtained. Keels which can flop about in the slot are not as efficient as rigid ones, and the crew of such a keelboat must check that the wedges are all in place before and after every race.

Spars should also be regularly examined, particularly at the halyard sheaves and attachment points of the rigging. Sheaves which have seized up will soon fall victim to the sawing action of wire halyards. I find that lightly graphited oil keeps them turning over well. Internal shroud fastenings are better because they eliminate snag points for the spinnaker, if nothing else, but it does make checking their attachment more difficult. Nevertheless this has to be done regularly, and also the spreader attachments to see that they are still rigid. In addition, it is most important to verify that the heel of the mast is in no way allowed to rotate as this alters the spreader angle. I have replaced the two pins in the mast step on my boat with a couple of three-sixteenths inch bolts done up very tightly, thus preventing distortion. To go a little further, I have drilled through the centre of the tenon of the mast step so that I can put a third bolt through it.

The boom is often neglected, and there's much a crew can do to clean it up. Take-off points for the main sheet and kicking strap are often clumsy. Both these and the under-boom tracks can be discarded—all that is needed is a one-eighth inch hole in the boom and a one-eighth inch 1 × 19 wire strop coming out of it for either purpose. A Talurit collar and a stainless steel washer provide the stop inside the boom. It must save nearly a pound in weight over the more conventional gear, and is a job within the capabilities of every crew.

The ends of standing rigging and points where it runs over spreaders or through deck bushes are vulnerable spots. If there is the slightest suspicion of the wire stranding or any broken strands it must be replaced immediately. Always take the old piece along for the rigger to match exactly. There is little permanent stretch in 1 × 19 rigging wire, but a quarter of an inch should be allowed in the average shroud.

Running rigging is most vulnerable where it runs over sheaves or around winches. I find that it needs renewing twice a year at least, and for that reason normally use galvanized wire rather than stainless steel. Stainless has the tendency to work harden, and then parts under tension without prior warning. Galvanized steel wire does start to show signs of deterioration by weeping rust. But whatever you do, don't accept galvanized rigging with copper ferrules on the Talurit splices—the corrosion is quite amazing. Galvanized wire is much easier to hand splice and every competent sailor should be capable of putting an eye splice in one-eighth flexible wire rope. He goes up one or two places in the skipper's eyes too if he can splice wire to rope. Neither is difficult, and it's the sort of job that can be accomplished in an armchair by the club bar, and usually to the psychological detriment of your rivals.

Sails, being the driving force of your boat, need constant care and attention. Never at any time should they be allowed to flap, as it destroys the individual fibres of the cloth and makes the sail deteriorate rapidly. Salt has to be rinsed out, and the sails should be dried lying on the grass. Crew and helmsmen should check for wear, particularly at the ends of the batten pockets and where chafe occurs from spreader ends, and on that line of the mainsail which is trapped between the boom and the shroud on a run. Minor repairs must be done as soon as they are needed. The super crew has his own bosun's bag with sail repair kit in it (Appendix D).

Trailers and trolleys need their regular maintenance too. It's easier to push the boat around on a well greased trolley, so why waste energy before you go afloat. It's all part of the crew's job to make sure the helmsman has done it; or else to do it himself.

With keelboats there are one or two nasty jobs. Slipping and scrubbing the boat is not exactly pleasant, but if you are to have any chance of success it must be done. True, a yard can be paid to do it, but I don't know a yard where the workers would give a boat the attention I would my own, so I do it myself. It's much easier with all hands helping, and no crew should ever try to excuse himself from this job. When the rules insist that the boat is kept afloat for the duration of a regatta there is no reason why the marine growths should get a hold on your perfect bottom finish. By diving with a face mask to scrub the bottom or as I saw at Kiel, using a six inch wide canvas strap passed under the boat and scrubbing the bottom with a sawing action, the early growth can be rubbed off before it has much adhesion.

For those who are looking for a quick way out on bottom preparation, I can only say that there is none, but you can improve on the natural cut-back paint a little. Graphspeed is a little easier to apply, but rubbing it down is the filthiest job I have ever undertaken. When properly burnished it does give a silky surface with a low surface tension coefficient with water, giving low drag. Hydron is a soft finish which needs no rubbing down after application; it leeches out a chemical which it is claimed noticeably reduces drag. It possibly adds a microfraction to boat speed, and it is a psychological weapon.

The importance of a well prepared and maintained boat cannot be over-emphasized. It is the crew's equal responsibility to see that everything is in peak condition and works. There is satisfaction in racing a good boat, and at least knowing that no one has any advantage over you.

3
Fitness

Like it or not, small boat racing is now an athletic sport. Ever since Paul Elvstrom demonstrated that with gymnasium training he could sit out for an entire race, the fact has slowly been accepted. When you no longer suffer physical discomfort, you are able to give your entire attention to getting to the finishing line first, but if it's painful much of your mental concentration is destroyed and the boat's performance is below par. Most races take between two and three hours and therefore demand stamina. Anyone who has hung over the side of a Soling in what is known as the 'mini-hike' position will know what stamina is at the end of a two-mile beat. Hanging in the most spine-destroying position ever devised in the name of pleasure for twenty-five minutes or so is not pleasant, but the ability to leap inboard at the weather mark, hoist the spinnaker and return to the mini-hike to trim it is all-important. The next 'rest' comes at the gybe mark, then there is another respite at the leeward mark before another twenty-five minutes of imitating a coal sack begins.

Suffering from back trouble at the end of 1971, I had fully intended to have a season's rest during the Olympic year and consequently had allowed that thickening around the waist that comes with idleness and good living. As a journalist I was going to see all the Olympic trials and the important regattas leading up to them. Just a few days before the first major Soling event I received a phone call from my old Hornet skipper Terry Wade, in need of a middle man for his campaign for the Olympics. He took the line that as I was going to be there anyway, wouldn't I rather see the racing from a competing boat? Naturally enough, I fell for it. I did warn him that he was taking on an unfit, spinally deformed cripple, but he took no notice. It was a compact campaign of three weeks' regattas with a week between each one, culminating in final trials at Poole. I was to be given a weekend to make up my mind— but that left me no way out since it was the weekend before the National Championship which started on the Monday! I was not unfamiliar with the Soling or to mini-hiking, but I was in no way fit enough to do it for more than two or three minutes without a break. There was no time to get fit and so I had to do it as we went along. By the time the trials were over I could just about last out for a whole race without my back giving me intense pain. This series of races was the one which I have least enjoyed in all the years I have been sailing, not because of the pain, but because I could not give one hundred per cent performance, and was thus reducing our overall race-winning potential.

Going back to the Hornet a couple of weeks after the Soling Olympic trials, I found life easy as I had reached a reasonable standard of physical fitness, and enjoyed the week's regatta to the full. Significantly, we were in the running for an overall win in this event, the World Championship, but lost the title to a team which had spent a lot more time preparing their boat and were thus able to show us the way home most of the time.

The demands on physical fitness are becoming greater. No longer is it good enough to be fit and heavy: now you lose weight for the lighter breezes and put it on with a weight jacket when it blows. Carrying one of these, weighing some twenty to twenty-five pounds, for a whole race is an energy-sapping effort which demands a greater level of fitness than ever before. Following the 1972 IYRU Conference, only classes which in their rules specifically allow the carrying of extra weight by the crews are allowed to carry on this practice; but most classes are falling into line with the wishes of their keener members and writing this prescription into their rules. Speed of movement too is of primary importance: reactions to changes in wind strength and direction are the most significant factors in winning. A fit crew can react faster and the boat benefits.

Not very long ago too much emphasis was being placed on gymnasium training. The best way to get fit for sailing is by more and more sailing. Though this is not always possible and a compromise has to be made, no amount of sitting out on a training bench pulling simulated sheets can replace half that amount of time spent sailing and developing the co-ordination that is so important. Nevertheless, the city-bound sailor will do his best to get fit in a gymnasium and maintain his fitness with a simple set of exercises at home. Ten minutes a day is not too much to ask of anyone, and almost every maintenance fitness course only requires this amount of endeavour.

Total concentration while racing is another hallmark of the good crew. In order to be able to achieve this the mind must be clear of all thoughts other than how to get to the finishing line first. It's not always easy to get rid of all the minor trials and tribulations of business and domestic life, but this is one of the basic concepts of leisure and one which must be mastered. A break in concentration when trimming the spinnaker will undoubtedly result in the sail collapsing and an irate yell from the back end of the boat as the helmsman's concentration is destroyed as well. The boat slows, places are lost, and it takes a long time before boat speed is back to normal. It can happen at any time anywhere on the course. Such lapses with their consequences cannot be tolerated, and therefore the mind must be trained to forget other run-of-the-mill problems while sailing.

Paul Elvstrom is perhaps more aware than most of the effect that psychological upsets can have on racing. He has always stressed the need to keep calm and have a clear mind, and believes that mental upsets cause the racing sailor to do stupid things which otherwise he might have avoided. There is little doubt that he was mentally upset at the 1972 Olympics and he withdrew before the end of the series. It may have been that, apart from one event, he has never done well at Kiel—this may have contributed further to his despondent attitude.

Mental blocks have to be cleared. I remember sailing a world championship dinghy event once with a helmsman who I felt was undergoing certain mental disturbance at the time. During practice we had a failure in our mast on which he effected a temporary repair. This repair was only good enough to hold out for half the first weather leg and the rest of the race had to be sailed nursing the sick spar. Since he was a spar manufacturer with five brand new spares on the trailer for the meeting, I could not understand this ostrich-like attitude. His reasoning was that the mast we had in the boat was tested, and none of the other five were. What he didn't seem to appreciate was that the one we were using was tested and found wanting.

I had a similar mental block when I first started crewing Hornets, and it was brought home in a much more dramatic fashion. I'd got it firmly in my head that the essence of a good tack was to have the jib hard home as quickly as possible at the expense of all else. My comeuppance came while crewing for Dick Pitcher at Burnham in a Force five easterly with a flood tide. We had a long beat with many tacks down the north shore of the Crouch. Dick told me that if I continued to tack like that we would capsize, but I took little heed. Sure enough, his words were soon borne out. I had got the jib pinned in on the new tack and had failed to get out on the sliding seat when a gust hit and the boat blew over. I learned my lesson, but I have a sneaking suspicion that Dick helped that capsize to stop me from my constant error. I thank him anyway for curing me of that habit.

Because the psychological relationships in small boat racing are of such importance, there is an entire chapter about the subject in this book. Peter Hunter combines the philosophies he has developed during his years of successful crewing with some perspicacious insights into the necessary psychology.

FITNESS TRAINING SCHEDULE

An adaptation of the Canadian 5BX plan is good enough for the average small boat sailor to maintain reasonable fitness. Some exercises should be avoided, particularly those which put too heavy strains onto the lumbar regions of the spine (toe touching is not as good as one might imagine). An osteopath friend recommends more gentle warming-up exercises and for this reason running on the spot should come first in any sequence. The main reason for the exercises is to keep the body supple; only hard work will increase muscle strength, but in the home muscle tone can be maintained.

The following schedule can be completed in ten minutes.

1. Running on the spot—300 (count each time right foot goes down).
2. Touching toe with opposite hand, lift to full stretch with hands raised above the head after having touched both—30.
3. Press-ups—20.
4. Sit-ups from prone position on back—30.
5. Lying face down with hands behind back, raise head and ankles together—30.
6. Stride jumps, raising hands level with shoulders—50.
7. Running on the spot—200.

Alternate days' exercise at this level is enough to maintain reasonable fitness, but starting from scratch the exercises must be done daily and built up from smaller levels. The falling off in physical ability due to age is more rapid than at first appreciated, but after twenty-five years the decline is marked and unless some form of fitness plan is adhered to regularly, the loss in sailing terms is considerable.

4
The Psychology and Philosophy of Crewing
by Peter Hunter

The attitude of competitors in small boat racing has changed markedly during the last twenty years. There has been a hardening of their approach, more specialization, a tremendous increase in technical knowledge; that elsewhere might be described as a professional outlook. To succeed in top competition it is imperative to stay one jump ahead of the opposition, but at the same time it must always be remembered that yacht racing is a sport—and as such should be enjoyed.

Crews, who necessarily bear the brunt of the work done in the boat, must enjoy what they are doing or they soon come into the category of 'used to be sailors'. It helps for the crew to believe that he is important. This can be achieved in two ways, by receiving praise from the skipper or taking over command. The latter is only for those who are streets better than the man at the helm, but the former is easy if the correct groundwork is put in. Skipper handling is an all-important attribute of the top crew. The crews who are constantly in demand will have mastered the attribute and will admit that it takes time to do so.

For some this psychological weapon may come naturally, but it would more normally be found in skippers. It is bred of an arrogance that comes with natural ability. Those fortunate enough to crew for a really good helmsman will readily appreciate the quality; those who crew for several will better develop their skipper handling. Receiving an invitation to crew for a good skipper is praise in itself, and the continuance of these invitations will show that the crew has begun to master the right approach. I found out about this when a rival skipper once congratulated my helmsman on his crew's 'low cunning': then, I realized that there was more to crewing than knowing all about sailing.

By all means experiment, but the basic principles must be observed. The skipper must be allowed to think that he is still in charge, although a nagging worry about it must help to sharpen him in the cut and thrust of actual competition. At no time should the situation be allowed to develop into acrimonious argument between skipper and crew. This only gives a psychological boost to the opposition; nothing is more encouraging to the crew of a chasing boat than the sound of a row going on in front. Concentration is being lost, and so are the yards of advantage. The crew must never resort to physical violence afloat; energies should be saved for dealing with the opposition.

To prevent any chance of acrimony, the choice of skipper made by the crew is important. First, he should be a man who commands the respect of the other skippers. In any other case the likelihood is that he will not have winning ways. In any dinghy park or club bar it is easy to pick out the successful skippers and with a little research confirm the selection. There is little point in crewing for a helmsman with little chance of winning. A good crew can lift a mid-fleet man somewhere into the hunt, but unless the skipper has the necessary flair and some skill, even the greatest crew is of only relative value.

Winning is all-important. Anything less is second class, but it is of paramount importance that racing should be enjoyed. These two factors should be impressed on the mind of every crew. Jasper Blount, a Swallow champion, impressed them on mine, and it was winning which came first to him. Olympic gold medallists find crews who put winning first; some crews have put up with their talented but testy skippers just as long as it was necessary to get their hands on the coveted medal and have then handed in their notice.

It's the crew's duty to put things into perspective. Too often a good idea in a helmsman's mind develops into a fetish. Then all reasoning disappears, all the good becomes undone, and the idea has a detrimental effect on the boat's performance. The crew who can view the effect objectively should keep his skipper aware of the pitfalls. I was caught up in the consequences of a fetish back in 1960 and at the time was too young to interfere. It was at the final Olympic trials for the Dragon class, which in true British fashion were held in the Bay of Naples (actually the scene of the Olympics), and because the middle man of Bruce Donald's *Penguin* dropped out with pathological seasickness I was recruited. A phobia over excess weight developed on board to the extent that if ever there was a spare second, a hand went onto the pump to drain the already dry bilges. The heat was intense and humid, yet because of the weight phobia we were only taking one pint of drinking water afloat with us. As the racing progressed our thirsts made us uncomfortable, we lost concentration and interest, and fell back down the fleet. The good crew would never have allowed that to happen; at the time I wasn't that good, and because of it failed to represent Britain in the 1960 Olympics.

The experienced crew, by dropping the odd phrase or name (not boastfully) can raise the standard of his skipper. In almost any sport the player raises his standard to the game in progress and this is just as true of yachting as any other. The man who has been crewing for an ace helmsman and finds himself with a mid-fleet man for a weekend can increase the team's chances of winning. I got my first sailing in a Flying Dutchman when I was crewing for Ralph Farrant, who at the time was very much at the front of the International 14 fleet. A good Osprey sailor, converted to FDs, invited me to crew him for a weekend at Whitstable. I was left over from the Prince of Wales week there and he had come alone for the Flying Dutchman series hoping to pick up a crew. Halfway through our first race, in which we were doing none too well, he asked who I had been crewing for. The name Ralph Farrant seemed to register sufficiently for him to begin to sail better. It brought home to me that great piece of crew psychology, that if the helmsman thinks the crew is better than him, he will try to sail up to the crew's standard.

Crews can destroy their skippers by irritating over-keenness. Too often it happens at a time of crucial concentration—the lead is yours and the closest rival one hundred yards behind on the final beat. A crew who has tensed himself up for a whole race can easily get twitchy in these circumstances. He may believe the sheeting to be all wrong and spend minutes fiddling with Barber hauler, sheets and Cunningham tensions, all the time muttering curses about his lack of success in getting things right. That sort of thing is calculated to drive away every bit of concentration from the skipper, and too often results in an easy win becoming a second place or worse.

Skippers vary in the way that they are best handled. Some need prodding or kicking all the way round the course. Try the same tactics with the type of helmsman who needs kid-glove handling and the results are disastrous. It is important, therefore, to understand the workings of the man at the back. His previous crews will generally indicate the sort of treatment that works; that far, fellow crews are prepared to help each other. The soft approach to the skipper is generally the most effective. Crews who really want something done either to the boat ashore or in a tactical situation afloat, have a better chance of realizing their aim if they make the skipper feel that the whole thing was his idea in the first place. The approach varies from one skipper to another and only experience will tell how the finesse should be applied.

Sailing a singlehander brings crewing fully into perspective. Crew and skipper being one provides a good working knowledge of what should go on at the back end of a dinghy, which any crew has to know to do his job well, but the privations of singlehanded sailing are not conducive to his well-being. Far better, therefore, for crews to get experience of helming two-man boats whenever possible. Good skippers appreciate the reasoning that the effect of bad crewing is felt at the back. Over-sheeting the spinnaker or jib, for example, make large amounts of rudder adjustment necessary, and each movement produces a braking effect. Any amount of heeling, either to windward or to leeward, does the same thing; but until crews get a full appreciation of how minor errors they make affect the overall boat speed they cannot become top class.

The worst type of skipper to deal with is the one who before the start is highly nervous. They are the best if handled correctly, but unless all systems are go before the boat is launched the crew has an impossible task. Their nervous energy must be channelled into the right direction—winning the race—and that is not difficult. Relaxing them is a crew's duty: whatever their hang-up afloat, it is not insurmountable. In the pre-race period the crew can talk about something of which the skipper has an encyclopaedic knowledge. I crewed once for a skipper with a double first in classics and somehow kept up a conversation about Attic Greek pronunciation until the ten minute gun. My own knowledge of the subject had to be researched beforehand, but I felt that this was part of the job of winning that particular series.

The crew must ask himself how far he is prepared to go in the rat race before embarking on a season's racing. Now it is patently clear that, contrary to the dictum of Baron Pierre de Coubertin, the Olympics are only for the 'professionals'. The expenditure of cash and time are too great for the happy amateurs, but there is still plenty of good racing to be had even in the six selected classes. The crew's own psychological problems cannot be maladjusted or he will never be able to exert his influence over the skipper, and that is part of crewing; a facet of the sport from which can be derived great pleasure and satisfaction. That pleasure and satisfaction can and should be heightened in two ways for the crew: nefariously, by knowing that he is in control, and introspectively, because the crew knows that he is really only a minor part in a major game. Humility has its advantage too. Crews should never fail to congratulate the man who beat them, but when they do so they should leave him in doubt as to whether they mean it.

A study in concentration in light weather. Note the fingertip grip on sheet and tiller.

5
Clothing and Personal Wear

When I started dinghy racing there were no really suitable clothes specially manufactured for the sport. If you look at pictures of the winners of big dinghy events in the magazines of twenty years ago you will find them in ordinary shirts with the sleeves rolled up and what looked remarkably like ex-Army baggy shorts. If it was colder they would have worn heavy oiled wool sweaters and maybe cotton twill anoraks.

I remember spending hours trying to waterproof a cotton anorak with a well-advertised product. It may have been some use in a rain shower, but not behind a full-blooded bow wave. Footwear, luckily, was one of the first things to be revolutionized. Several manufacturers produced specially soled canvas shoes in the late 1940s and since then they have tried to better their sailing shoes. Short boots followed soon after, and now there is a choice which should satisfy everyone.

The first oilskins for dinghy sailors came in the form of a yellow PVC smock and separate trousers, both voluminous. Now there is a wide choice, and no need for anyone to go afloat resembling a refugee from a jumble sale. Pressure has been brought to bear on manufacturers to produce good clothes which are both efficient for the job and durable.

In the North European climate a wet suit is essential to efficient sailing. I wonder how we used to get on without them, and have memories of going sailing loaded down with extra trousers and sweaters until I resembled the Michelin man. The one-piece wet suit has most to recommend it, since it has less things to catch on than the rest. Zips at the ankles and wrists are unnecessary, and again only provide something more for gear to snag on. My own suit is three millimetre neoprene with nylon towel lining and a nylon outer covering. It has one nylon zip from crutch to neck. For most of the year I wear this and a pair of tight shorts to protect the suit at the point of major wear. In the depths of winter I augment the insulation by wearing an additional pair of jeans and a sweater and, to keep the whole lot under control, a nylon overall.

When the weather shows a marked improvement I swop my full wet suit for a 'shortie' which just covers the body, and wear shorts and a tee shirt and nylon spray jacket over it. One day someone is going to tell all the manufacturers of spray jackets not to provide them with a hood which can never be used and which only gets in the way of the kicking strap and other rigging and creates windage. I have had to cut them off my jackets for years now, ever since I lost a special one that Seahorse Sails made for me years ago. Velcro has made a great difference in the fastenings of sailing clothes, eliminating zips which corrode and jam. Most of the better garments use it for cuffs, ankles and fronts.

Whenever I have had the opportunity to sail in sunnier climes I have experimented with clothes. Western Australians sail in nothing but a pair of shorts, a tee shirt and a spray jacket. This is fine if your skin is ready for the strong overhead sun, but when I did a fortnight's championship racing out there I was certainly not prepared after leaving mid-winter London for mid-summer Perth. The heat as well as the sunshine was a problem. I got over both by wearing light trousers, a tee shirt and white cotton twill jacket. When this jacket got wet it acted like a refrigerator as the spray evaporated from it in the wind, keeping me cool inside it. This was all right for the duration of the race, but I did feel chilly on the sail home. Wearing identical jackets, one or two of the other British competitors complained of cold and wore wet suit jackets under them.

But even more important than warmth in this sort of climate is the protection from sun. On the way to the starts and on the sail home a hat with a big brim to keep as much sun off the face is the best possible protection. Sun tan cream is a must, and over the nose, cheekbones and ears, where the high sun burns most, barrier cream is essential. In Perth the locals use white zinc oxide paste, as it's cheap and more effective than anything else. People using it look like a Red Indian raiding party, but they do save themselves from intense discomfort. When I was out there it seemed stupid not to follow the locals' advice—if they used it, and they were hardened to the sun, it would have been suicide for us not to.

Australians also tend to sail small boats in their bare feet, but unless the water is very warm this is not a practice I recommend. Stubbing a toe can be painful, and it would certainly slow you down for a critical second or two. When questioned, many of the barefoot brigade say it is for grip, but the latest sailing shoes are equal in every way to bare feet. The modern laced short boot with protection patches for toestrap wear are perhaps the best there is.

One of the newer items of sailing clothing is the polar suit. This looks like a track suit but on the inside has about a quarter inch of nylon fur. One of these worn next to the skin provides a perfect dry insulation layer, similar to a wet suit but without its restrictiveness. Under a nylon overall it is ideal for keelboat sailing in almost any weather.

Try to avoid hats whenever possible, though in winter a woollen cap is useful. If you keep your head warm, it is medically acknowledged that your brain works faster, but I think this is the only time they are necessary. Normally, hats provide windage and tend to blow off. Added to which they stop you from feeling the change in strength of the wind on the back of your neck.

In strong sun, particularly when it is low on the horizon, a pair of Polaroid sunglasses may help. They are particularly useful when trimming a spinnaker when the sun is right on the luff (and how often it is). They are a help, too, when looking up-sun for a mark. Try not to wear them all the time, but keep them handy in the boat. One pair should be sufficient between the helmsman and crew. Silicone polish on the glasses helps to get rid of the spray quickly, but this needs redoing before each race.

Gloves are not just a sissy way of looking after hands. They provide sensible protection against blisters and soreness which adds to one's efficiency. When Tony Morgan first started to crew with Keith Musto in a Flying Dutchman, after a weekend's racing his hands looked like raw meat; after a championship week you needed a strong stomach to look at them. Tony was one of the first crews I knew to use gloves. He started with thick household rubber ones, and tried almost everything within reach. Its perhaps a little more than coincidental that his former helmsman Keith Musto now produces some of the very best sailing gloves on the market. They have soft leather palms doubled where the wear is greatest and nylon net backs. The cut-off fingers maintain the sensitivity of the finger tips. Using gloves, sheet sizes for both jib and spinnaker can be cut down and the weight saving is considerable. The action of gloves is simply to add a buffer

What the well dressed crew is wearing. An all-over elasticated nylon suit covering buoyancy aid and trapeze harness, with only the hook showing. (*Guy Gurney*)

layer over the skin: see how quickly the leather wears out and then consider what might have happened to the hands inside them. Gloves made out of wet suit material do not even last one race. Those with full-length fingers are pretty useless as they prevent gear adjustments, undoing shackles or fiddling with the spinnaker pole ends. Buy the best and save yourself frustration and money.

To summarize, the ideal clothing keeps out the cold, is light and tight fitting, but allows freedom of movement. It does not have any metal buckles, buttons or zips, and it is made of materials which are tear resistant. It seems that the better the quality (and therefore generally the higher the price), the longer it will last.

The majority of dinghies now have a trapeze; there are plenty of different types of trapeze belt on the market and I consider these as part of the crew's clothing. Anyone who has used one will know how important it is to have one that fits comfortably. If in any way you don't come within the range of normal sizes, it's as well to have one tailor-made to fit you—the extra cost will be amply repaid in its use. When I think of the first trapeze harnesses that were made in the early days and had to be adapted to be of any use, I shudder. They were of webbing and literally little more than a waistband with a hook or gate latch to connect to the wire. Then came the 'nappy' type which forced its wearer to use two hands to connect it to the trapeze wire and was a waste of time. Support for the back and shoulders was unthought-of, and kidneys took an immeasurable pasting. I'm sure it was only after someone had taken more punishment than he could stand that more sensible trapeze harnesses with shoulder straps and ample protection around the kidneys began to appear. These improved harnesses, now readily available, help to give better balance on the gunwale. The height of the hook on the body is crucial, and it should only be a couple of inches or so above the centre of gravity of your body for efficient trapezing (Colin Turner has more to say on this in a separate chapter). Many off-the-shelf harnesses are good, but a word of warning before buying. Try it on first and don't hesitate to make alterations to suit yourself.

Musto & Hyde were the first on the market with a weight jacket. To some people this would be an implement of torture, but with it a crew can add nearly twenty-five pounds (11 kg) where it helps most. The jacket, which is made of several layers of blanket inside a porous nylon quilted cover, can be soaked in water to increase crew's efficiency in stronger breezes. With the soaking material controlled within a jacket, extra weight is taken on in a much handier way than by loading on umpteem soggy old sweaters which hang loose around the waist and drag in the water. The weight jacket with its three quick-release strap fastenings is easy to get out of in the water, and by taking it off the crew will not find it difficult to climb back on board. However, before anyone uses one, he must be aware that he has to be really fit to carry this extra twenty-five pounds all the way round a course. It's not for nothing that they were quickly dubbed 'death jackets' by those who were forced to wear them by over-zealous helmsmen. Now they are a regular tool of the crew's trade.

6
Pre-Race Procedures

As a rule helmsmen tend to try to avoid the physical side of boat preparation before the start. It all gets left to the crews, who when they have a few spare moments to check up on the paperwork should have the necessary details ready for the skipper when he finds himself in a predicament. The good crew will carry the burden of rigging the boat and yet also know all there is to know about the course and conditions.

Travelling to an open meeting some distance from home needs preparation. The crew must ensure that the boat is properly loaded on the trailer, that all the lashings are secure, and that there are no loose bits that can get lost on the way. Put the heel of the mast together with all the shroud ends, halyards etc. inside an old sail bag so that none of the vital little bits and pieces can get lost. Unfortunately for me, one day the sail bag I was using split and I had a trail of rope about fifty feet behind the boat until a passing motorist flagged me down.

Skipper and crew should check that they have everything likely to be needed. Sails and battens, paddle, kedge, spinnaker poles are all easily left behind. One of the most easily forgotten items is the measurement certificate, and the race committee are then bound to want to see it. For a championship, it is as well to do a complete check that the boat still measures. Black bands are easy to check and sails should always be measured before every big meeting. If the crew remembers all these things, there should be no major worries before they arrive. The final check is to make sure that the tool box is packed, because the rest of the fleet are a trifle fed up with the people who are constantly borrowing tools.

During the week previous the best preparation is to find out everything possible about the place where the race is going to take place. A chart is often very revealing about tidal flow, and to some extent the pattern of wind bends can be predicted by examining the coastal topography. This, and the time of the start, are all-important; the former as a conversation topic for crew and helmsman on the journey, the latter so that they leave home in good time.

Arriving at the club, it is important to get down to work straight away. The boat should be parked as close to the slipway as possible and unpacked from the trailer. Put all the trailer lashings, lights and strongbacks into one large bag and get it stowed in the car. The boat is off-loaded onto the launching trolley and the helmsman goes away to park the trailer and to the race office. There he has to collect race instructions which he should bring back to the boat. While he is away the crew can proceed undisturbed to rig the boat.

The first job is to wash down the bottom to remove all the dirt thrown up on the journey. Since crew and helmsman have probably spent many hours producing a good finish it would be a shame not to take advantage of it. The job only takes five minutes with a bucket of detergent and a sponge and a flick over with a hose afterwards. It's worth doing it before every race: just see how much muck there is on the bottom of a dinghy in the morning, particularly if it has rained hard—the dirt bounces up and sticks quite firmly. Keelboats should also be thoroughly washed before being craned into the water. If they have been sitting on a mooring for more than a day they need a rub over with a sponge or the canvas strap treatment described earlier. By the time the crew has finished this task the helmsman should have returned to give him a hand to step the mast.

Before the mast is put in the boat it is absolutely essential to check that everything is in the right place, that the wind indicator is fixed to the top, and that none of the halyard ends are in the upper sheaves. Too many times I have seen people omit to check and then have to take the mast out again or pull the boat over on its side, risking damage to the hull, to put things right.

Once the mast is up, the helmsman can sit down with the race instructions while the crew gets on with rigging. He will check over each piece of gear as he goes, examine the fairleads and lead blocks for all the control lines to make certain they are not worn or seized, check the cam jam cleats to make sure both cams work properly, look at the lines to see if they are frayed or that they are not coming adrift at the ends, and see that there is no play at the mast step before taping up all the pins. Then he will check that the whole rig is properly set up before attempting to put the sails on.

The helmsman should now double-check everything the crew has done, before he selects the sails for the day. This can take some time if he has more than one suit. While he makes up his mind, the crew can familiarize himself with the race instructions before stowing them in the boat. He must make a note of the time of the tide—not just a mental note, but written down. In my boat I have one or two small Chinagraph pencils attached to the deck with Velcro; they are near pieces of white Fablon (plastic) stuck on the deck, and on these I write the tactical information. Tide time is one of the first to be included after the starting time. Any information related to the tide time, such as the change of flow, is also noted. That way it is there for reference and no one has to memorize it.

One thing the crew should wise up on in the sailing instructions is whether there is any safety tally to take out, or a sheet to sign on as a starter, or a declaration to sign and by what time it has to be done. It is quite useless putting everything into a race only to throw it all away on a technicality, and the responsibility for seeing that these things are done is equally the crew's. I once lost a quart mug—the only one I have ever had the chance of winning—because my helmsman failed to sign the declaration. Luckily it was only the practice race of a World Championship, but it was as much my fault as his that I don't drink out of a quart mug today. From that day on I have always pestered my helmsman as soon as we get ashore to sign his declaration. I honestly believe that it is a waste of time and should be totally abolished— there were no declarations at the 1972 Olympics—but its protagonists are still in the majority where it counts.

While most people know their own class flag, it is worth checking that the sailing instructions have not altered it; if so the crew must know what its replacement looks like. He must also know what all the flag signals mean. In the heat of the battle it is the crew who has to keep his eyes peeled for them. (Appendix C gives details of the standard signals.)

Quite often there are local rules which don't immediately appear logical, but which are no doubt based on sound sense. For instance, there may be some buoy which boats are always required to pass on the seaward side; it could be because there is an underwater obstruction inshore. Whatever the reason, the crew must be aware of the regulation or pay the consequences.

A practice sail well before the race is well worth while;

should anything go wrong then there is time to correct it. It will also give the opportunity of getting settled into a rhythm with the helmsman and for both to turn the landmarks and buoys on the chart into visible realities. Crews will find that they have to encourage their helmsman into going afloat without actually racing, but it's really worth the effort. This could be one of those times when they swap places and try each other's job.

Before going afloat for the race the crew should get a last minute check on the weather forecast. It doesn't cost much to phone the local meteorological station and get an up-to-date synopsis. The better newspapers publish a general synoptic chart, and by following these and television forecasts in advance of the day a good crew can build a forecasting technique of his own. If the wind is going to shift during the course of the race, and it can be predicted, and the crew does it, his value will increase immeasurably. When I worked full time for BBC Television my office was three doors away from the weatherman's. I never failed to nip in there on Friday evening to find out the expected weather pattern for wherever I was going for the weekend. If there is an advantage on your doorstep it is foolish not to take it.

The final check should be for things that are needed in the boat. Many years ago I heard Beecher Moore say that you should never go afloat without a knife, a length of codline and a shackle. If the damage cannot be repaired with one or all of these it's probably too bad to try to carry on anyway. Many a race has been saved for me by carrying the 'Beecher pack', so I check that I've got that and then look for the rest of the tools. In a dinghy these do not amount to more than a screwdriver and a pair of pliers, but as the size of the boat increases so does the size and number of tools. When I was crewing in C class catamarans I never went to sea without a set of Mole Grips and a shifting spanner.

The protest flag must also be in the boat. Whether or not you like them, protests are very much part of racing. To get one heard you must fly a flag, and International Code B is always acceptable. I did hear of one European race committee that was so pedantic that it threw out one protest because the flag didn't have the swallowtail cut in. That would have stuck in my throat like a fishbone, because the swallowtail in International Code B is only optional.

If you are going to be afloat for more than a couple of hours it is best to take something to eat and drink. There is nothing worse than dehydration, and a plastic bottle of orange squash is the complete answer. In addition an easily digested glucose-packed chocolate or candy bar helps. Eating one of these about twenty minutes before the start has a two-fold effect: it breaks into the nervous tension and then provides a good source of energy. On a long sail home after the race a can of fizzy lemonade is a good thirst quencher after a dry-mouthed finish. Store the goodies at the front of the boat and then the crew can play the conjuring tricks at the right moment—he'll find it does have an interesting and useful purpose, as it often softens the helmsman.

The sailing instructions are kept on board, but before going afloat the crew must check the noticeboard for any last minute alterations, and if there are note them down with the Chinagraph.

For success, get off good and early. Slipways are generally clear for the first ones afloat. It's as well to be in the region of the start with nearly an hour to go if crew and helmsman are to have a chance to settle down and get their pre-start checks all sorted out.

The critical moment just after the start. Bev Moss on the wire helps Derek
Farrant to drive away fast into clear air.

7
The Start

For the benefit of the crew, the skipper should sail gently to the starting area after launching or casting off the mooring, taking it easily so that the crew can get the gear sorted out and stowed. Halyard falls must be packed away neatly or in no time they will produce a cat's cradle in the front cockpit. A small Terylene bag fixed to a deck beam just forward of the mast or the forward bulkhead into which the halyard falls are packed saves a lot of trouble. One with two compartments can also double as the bosun's store for a knife, shackles, pliers, screwdriver and a couple of lengths of codline.

Once everything is ship-shape, helmsman and crew must begin to sail hard in order to settle down to a rhythm. This is as important in a keelboat where the crew may only be hanging over the side giving the appearance of a coal sack while beating, but tacking and manoeuvring are all better after a little practice.

From almost an hour before the start the crew should be jotting down compass readings on both tacks and the true wind direction at ten minute intervals. Only by doing this can he see if there is any pattern in the wind movement. He should take all the readings close to the starting line, in order to have them non-variable. However, it is important to sail up to the weather mark and see if there is any significant difference in the wind direction up there. Wind bends are more important than shifts, and any prior knowledge of their existence puts that team one-up on the opposition.

When I sailed with Terry Wade in the British Soling Championships in Torbay in 1972 we were almost always the first ones out on the course, sometimes up to an hour and a half before the start. We were then able to sail all over the bay and check on the wind direction. Before one particular race we found a very big wind bend right on the edge of our course. It paid to go a little further into this than appeared necessary and carry a close reach to the weather mark. We checked it again with twenty minutes to go and hustled back to the starting line determined to start at the end nearer our favourable bend. Straight after the start we tacked on to port and headed towards the shore. In good time we got the header and held on for awhile until we were nearly thirty degrees off our original heading. Then we tacked and were able to start our sheets as we romped towards the weather mark. We got there with a comfortable lead which we held on the two reaches, and so we started on the second beat once again heading for our wind bend. It surprised us that no one followed up, particularly after our first beat success. As it was, on that leg we dropped to sixth as two hefty windshifts in the middle of the bay destroyed our advantage. When they occurred we had sailed out of their zone of effect. We should have covered our opposition and not been greedy, but had anyone else gone for our bend then we should have gone with them. Our initial advantage was certainly due to our hard work before the race started.

Crews must know how to read the compass and call the lifts and headers in the wind to the helmsman as he has other things on which to concentrate. For this reason the compasses should be mounted so that both can see them. Rodney Pattisson has started a trend to have two compasses on each side of the boat so that the crew can get an even better view.

All such pre-race information should be jotted down on the tactical boards with a Chinagraph pencil, particularly the heading on each tack. These are important as they give an instant check on whether the boat is lifted or headed on a tack. An increase in the bearing in degrees on starboard tack indicates a lift, and a fall-off in the bearing, a header. Conversely, on port tack as the bearing gets smaller in number the boat is freed, and headed if the bearing becomes larger.

Take a compass bearing of the starting line and jot that down too. These bearings must be clearly marked near the compasses. Take bearings on the windward mark from the leeward one, and at the same time the wing mark. The importance of going to the weather mark can not be too highly stressed as from there another bearing of the wing mark can be obtained. They may be shown on the committee boat, but it always pays to check.

On an Olympic type course at a major regatta the likelihood is that the committee boat will display the bearing to the weather mark; from this the other bearings can be calculated. From the weather mark to the wing mark on a port hand course deduct 135 degrees from the first bearing. From the wing mark to the leeward mark deduct a further 90 degrees. As a check deduct another 135 degrees to see that the original figure for the first beat comes up. For starboard courses these figures should be added. It is the crew's duty to check that these bearings are correct as he will have to give them to the skipper at each mark, and the possibility is that for half the leg these will be the only directional guide he has if there is a lot of water flying around or a sea mist to hide the marks.

I cannot stress too fully the importance of these compass bearings. Before the days of compasses in dinghies, I was racing in the Hornet World Championships on the Ijselmeer from Muiden with Reg White. A lot depended on the last race in the series, but almost all the competitors threw it away. The course was a triangle with a right angle from the windward leg to the wing mark. The start and finish was halfway up the windward leg and the course was port handed. Shortly after the start the wind freed the fleet on port tack, but as it was a grey misty day the shoreline was obscured, and no one realized just how much this wind shift was. Consequently, when we got to the windward mark we all sailed off on a beam reach to where we expected to find the wing mark. We sailed for a long time and found nothing, yet still none of us had twigged what had happened. Eventually, we found a buoy and rounded that, but it turned out to be the wrong one. What had happened was that the second leg had turned into a close fetch on starboard tack because of the windshift. Only Marten Van Mesdag with Dudok Van Heel and Beecher Moore and his wife Bobbie found the correct wing mark that day. They thought it out, but had we had compasses the outcome could have been very different.

While sailing back from the weather mark before the start the spinnaker should go up. It allows a final check that none of the gear is snarled up, which is a positive certainty if there has been a last minute jib change and the spinnaker is stowed in a launcher chute. It is far better to find out before the race than have an irate helmsman shortly after the weather mark.

Get back near the line with twenty minutes to go and have something to eat and drink that is easily digestible and supplies plenty of energy. It pays not to go far from the line, and to make sure the helmsman has the good manners to keep out of the way of classes starting earlier. It is not only good manners, it is sound public relations. One never knows when he might want a favour when racing from one of these boats, like a clearance on a close tack on port across their bows.

When there is not much wind about the crew should make certain that the helmsman does not get downtide of the line. There is little point in getting out good and early if your chances are ruined by not being able to start in the right place. The mooring chain on the committee boat provides an accurate indicator of how the tide is running; it pays to check this at the other end of the line as well. The crew must be able to provide his skipper with every bit of information that is useful, because at this stage tension is building for the man at the helm.

After years of experimenting with all sorts of systems I have finalized what I consider to be the best way to get the best start. The watch should be with the crew, since in the last minute before the start the helmsman needs all the attention he can give to getting in the right place on the line and avoiding all the other boats around. He has not got time to look down at the watch and must rely on the crew to give him the time. Hitting the line with the gun is all-important; a second late can instantly mean the second rank of the fleet. The average racing dinghy travels half its length in a second when going to windward flat out, it is a little less for keelboats. For catamarans it is as much as a whole boat length every second.

Ideally the crew should have a waterproof stopwatch on a wrist strap. Those hung around the neck on bits of string are quite useless since the watch has to be turned over to see it. Unfortunately, I have yet to come across a really efficient waterproof stopwatch. After a very short time the stem glands go around the stop and start buttons and water gets in. I use my wristwatch which I know to be waterproof, with a Chinagraph pencil. At the ten minute gun I mark on the glass of the watch the position of the sweep second hand and the position where the minute hand will be in ten minutes' time. By the marks I put an S and an M to avoid confusing the two. When the five minute gun goes I get a more accurate check on the seconds and re-do the Chinagraph mark. It is cheaper and just as accurate as a stopwatch, it's more reliable because the watch is waterproof, and not as chancy as a rotating bezel as it cannot get moved accidentally. It also takes the chance element out of one's memory, and when the pressure is on this is the first thing that is likely to go.

While the countdown is going on the helmsman should be sailing up and down the line making his final evaluation of its

bias and deciding which end to start on. Most times he will
have discussed this with the crew beforehand, but it must be
checked in case a last minute wind change alters the bias on the
line. There is one sure way of determining which end of the
line to start. Sail down the line with the jib flapping or furled
and mainsail just lifting, and then turn round and sail back the
other way. If the mainsail lifts more on the return leg the best
start is from the end to which the boat is now pointing. If it
does not lift, the other end is the place to start. There has to be
an enormous port tack bias before starting on that tack has any
value, because any boat that does has to cross the pack of
starboard tack right-of-way boats, and unless there is a very
heavy bias this will be impractical.

What the helmsman aims for is to hit the starting line with
full way on and nobody affecting his wind. It is particularly
important not to have anyone stuck on the leeside, and a little
ahead, even more important than having a boat level to
windward. It is vital that the crew should appreciate all the
nuances of starting technique in order to understand the
skipper's various manoeuvres. If the helmsman is unwittingly
making a major error the crew can then draw attention to his
mistake with some authority.

The crew keeps the countdown going all the time from the
ten minute gun, in minutes until the five and then in half
minute intervals until two minutes to go. When he calls 'two
minutes' he checks that the centreboard is fully down and that
the jib sheets are not tangled or fouled. He then tells the
skipper the quarter minutes until there is one minute left,
when he counts down every five seconds. For the final fifteen
seconds it is every second until the gun. Counting down should
be done so that only your own skipper can hear. Make it clear,
but not so loud that every other helmsman in the vicinity can
hear, otherwise they will benefit from your efforts and that's
not the idea. On one occasion I did count down loudly, but
that was done deliberately and early. I was sailing with Reg
White in the prototype Tornado catamaran and we noticed a
large bunch at the weather end where we wanted to be. I
agreed with Reg that I would count down five seconds early.
That threw our rivals into some confusion: some started early
and had to come back. We got in behind the front rank and
tacked immediately onto port and were away clear of the fleet.
It is a tactic that only works once in a lifetime, but beware of
anyone trying to pull it on you.

From the moment the gun goes the crew has got to put his
all into making the boat go as fast as it will. Those early
minutes are critical; the majority of races are won and lost at

this stage. It is essential to listen for the recall and to tell the skipper if the boat's number is among them. No crew should have much idea whether his boat was over—he should have been concentrating on the watch. The skipper will want an eye kept on the boats around and to know if there are any likely to affect him. He will need to know well in advance so that he can plan his strategy.

This is a nerve-racking time when it is easy to over-sheet the jib. With all the air being cut up by the close proximity of the fleet it will not be possible to sail as close to the true wind as normally. It will pay to drive off fast and free in order to get clear wind. To encourage the skipper, make certain the jib is eased a fraction and draw his attention sharply every time he is pinching. The crew must sit out hard so that the boat is bolt upright and then the skipper will be bound to sail free; if the boat heels he will tend naturally to pinch. The crew should encourage the skipper with phrases like 'you're killing 'em skip', or 'she's moving nicely today'. He'll know if he is doing well, and he won't need any telling if he's not, but the odd bit of encouragement can help at this crucial stage.

Photographs of starts show that there is always crowding near the ends because there it is easier to place the boat relative to the line. In the majority of starts the fleet hangs well back in the middle, as far as two lengths short of the line. The crew can encourage his skipper into this free space, where he can start with completely clear air and freedom to tack when he wants. It has to be timed very accurately, and any boat attempting it must only break clear of the pack with ten seconds to go or they will take a bunch with them.

Approaching the line, there are times when the skipper will want to take way off the boat. He can do it by just easing the mainsheet, but at times he will need the jib eased or even backed (i.e. sheeted to windward); he may require the plate raised to make leeway. When he wants these things done he is always a second late in calling for them, so the crew must anticipate his demands and be ready to fulfill them in an instant. However, he must never take the initiative in the few minutes before the start. He should feed his helmsman all the information he can and encourage him towards the line, but he should never sheet in too soon. The man at the helm should know what to do: if he doesn't, he should be told—after the race is over.

Most club starts are unlikely to be dead to windward, and while there is then some variation of the helmsman's starting technique there is little change in the crew's duties and the basic principles outlined here still apply.

8
The Windward Leg

Too many crews are under the misguided impression that their role on the windward leg is purely as shifting ballast. These are the non-contributing crews, destined at the best to a mediocre sailing life in the middle of the fleet. Of course weight and how it is used is important, but it is only one of the factors that the crew can contribute towards getting his boat first to the windward mark. Yacht racing demands a combination of mental and physical skills and effort and the thinking crew is the one who is likely to be the most use.

Having got clear wind after the start, the fastest way to the weather mark is by keeping as close to the median line of the wind direction as possible; that is, by tacking each time the wind heads. This plus careful use of the fair tide or avoidance of a foul one is most likely to get a boat to the front of the fleet. Wind bends over the course must also be considered and strategy planned accordingly. This strategy will have been discussed between crew and helmsman before the start, and the crew must be prepared to make minor alterations to meet conditions as they alter. The well balanced team splits the duties so that each person can concentrate harder on the job in hand. One of the best arrangements is to let the skipper concentrate on getting every bit of boat speed that he possibly can, trimming the sails (calling for any jib alternation that he wants), steering through the waves and driving it hard. The crew can then act as an information service, telling him of windshifts (by watching the other boats and the gusts on the water to windward), of the wind bends (by watching the compass), and of the tactics. To be able to make this sort of split, helmsman and crew must have implicit mutual trust. No crew can expect to take over this role within weeks of starting sailing: to be really efficient he has to be able to helm the boat nearly as well as his skipper. He can contribute right from the start if he is prepared to give the helmsman informed comment on what the other boats are doing. Informed comment only—not a constant stream of idle chatter.

In light weather and smooth water it pays to let the boat heel to leeward slightly so that most of the weather side of the hull comes out of the water and reduces the wetted area. The crew should also sit well forward to lift the stern and ease the flow of water from around it. The same is true for keelboats, and there is another advantage in very light weather in allowing or encouraging heeling to leeward and that is that the weight of the sailcloth helps the sail to set properly. Under these conditions, the boat will be pointed quite high and mainsail and jib can be sheeted closer to the centreline, but with the sheets eased a small amount to encourage flow in the sails.

Tacking in light weather can be wearisome, but there is no doubt that the roll tack does pay handsome dividends. It takes co-ordination between helmsman and crew that can only come with practice. The crew's job is to maintain the heel of the boat on the new tack as the helmsman changes sides. From the beginnings of the roll tack the sequence is: the helmsman puts the helm to leeward at the same time as he sits out quite violently to windward. As the water touches his backside, and the boat comes through the eye of the wind, the helmsman makes a quick movement to the other side—that's when the crew maintains the balance. When he gets across he will correct the amount the boat has over-heeled. The action of rolling the boat to windward increases the flow of air across the sails and gives the extra forward power to go through the tack. In absolutely still conditions forward progress can be made by putting in one roll tack after another; however, anyone trying it will be disqualified under Rule Number 60 which states that the boat shall be propelled by the '*natural* action of the wind upon the sails'. And it's not just dinghies that benefit from roll tacking: keelboats do as well, and then the crew has to help the helmsman with the roll and not simply counterbalance his movement.

When tacking in light weather, it is easy to kill the boat by jerking the jib fully home as she comes on the new tack. It should be pulled in gently so that the boat is helped to accelerate away. This maxim is true for all types of boats, and is only modified slightly as the wind increases in that the jib sheet comes in just a little quicker. Nothing stops a boat faster

Right in the middle of the tack, but the crew has been slow. The genoa is not free from the old tack yet the mainsail has started to draw on the new tack. Good tacking is particularly important in up-river conditions.

than jerking the sheets. Every effort should be made not to let the jib go free until it has started to lift. The initial part of tacking puts increased flow across the sails and it should be used to speed the boat through the tack.

Control of the jib sheet during the tack is so important that it makes me give dubious consideration to the self-tacking jib systems now prevalent on boats like Solings and Stars. True they do have a fine sheet control that can be played, but I have seen very few coarse jib sheet controls rigged to either side of the boat where they need to be, to be used properly. With this system on a fast-tacking keelboat like the Soling or the Star there is one great advantage, that the crew in any reasonable breeze can be in the mini-hike position before the full force of the wind is in the sails, since they do not have the problem of winching the jib home. But unless they trim the jib with the fine sheet control I think that much of the advantage is lost.

In bigger waves it is important to maintain good boat speed so that the boat is not stopped. The crew has now got to put the physical effort into keeping the boat flat. In moderate winds it will be a constant change from in to out and back again as the strength varies, but movements must be catlike and it is important to anticipate the wind. Gusts make a pattern on the water, and the crew must be prepared to move out just before they hit so that the boat does not heel to leeward. Similarly, the quieter patches of wind can be seen on the water and the crew must anticipate the lulls and be ready to come in so that the boat does not heel to windward.

Helmsman and crew will sit further aft in bigger waves in order to get the stem up and over the crests with the boat as upright as possible. The wetted surface is not as important under these conditions as boat control and maximum forward drive from the rig. Because of the waves not all the hull will be immersed at any time.

The action of getting a dinghy or a keelboat to windward in a seaway is to luff up the face of the wave and bear away through the trough. The crew's job is to keep the boat absolutely upright throughout the movement. It will mean sitting out a little harder as the helmsman bears away each time and moving in a fraction as he luffs. As the wind gets stronger and the boat is overpowered the helmsman should set up his sheets for the lightest point of the wind and then when a gust hits he and the crew must sit out that little bit harder. On a trapeze this is the time to throw your hands above your head to get every bit of weight as far outboard as possible. The helmsman will then ease the mainsheet, but the extra effort of the crew on the wire has minimized the boat's heel at a crucial

Going to windward in light weather, the crew watching forward for other boats likely to catch them on port tack and for any windshifts on the water while the skipper concentrates on the sails. A pair of sunglasses might have prevented the necessity to squint.

moment, and it will have gained forward speed and not made leeway.

All the time when going to windward the crew must read the compass. He will have already noted the mean heading on each tack on the tactical boards in Chinagraph. As soon as they have settled down on the tack he should inform the skipper how the boat is pointing, if it is freed or headed and by how much. The skipper is bound to smile if there is a freer at the beginning of a tack and again if there is a header where he wants to tack. What he doesn't want is a header just after he's tacked, but if this is a fact the crew must not withold it. The crew is not there to boost his helmsman's ego or sublimate his peace of mind; just to help him to win races.

At all times the crew must keep his eyes peeled for boats in the vicinity, particularly those who may cross ahead or force his boat about when on port tack. The particular boat to watch for when on starboard tack is the one who, if he judges it nicely, can tack on the lee bow. If the crew leaves his hail until the point where the other boat will have to tack instantly, it is likely he will then be in some confusion because of a quick tack and more than likely the defending boat will sail straight through the attacker's weather.

One of the worst possible things that can happen when tacking in a big seaway is that a wave hits the boat just as it tacks. This will stop it so dead that several lengths are lost before full way is regained. The tack may not even be made at all. If, therefore, the crew sees his skipper about to put them in this position he should tell him and try to prevent it.

Crew and skipper must have some sort of regular warning worked out so that the crew knows exactly when they are going to tack. There is nothing worse than the crew getting left behind in this manoeuvre, particularly if he is on a trapeze. A 'ready about' followed by a 'lee-oh' a couple of seconds later is fine; it gives the crew time to unjam the jib sheet and prepare himself. Once, when I was sailing a Hornet with John Partridge, we had after a couple of seasons achieved a remarkable rapport in our sailing. I knew exactly when he was going to tack and why. Consequently, the warning system got dropped and nothing was said. One day, for no apparent reason, he tacked. I hadn't seen this tack coming and was caught napping. Certain acrimonious discussions took place when I did get to the other side of the boat. For the next tack I got a very loud and slightly sarcastic warning; by the following one we were back in the old routine. I wasn't asleep: I just did not think he should have tacked there and then. We argued about it afterwards and I've a sneaking suspicion that my thoughts were right, but I would never press it. It takes a lot of sailing together to get a rapport like that, and even then it can so easily go wrong.

Gusts that do not alter the direction of the wind but only increase its strength do have a fan effect preceding them, causing a slight header before the gust and another as it dies. No one should be fooled into thinking that they should tack as they get the first header. Most windshifts can be read by the pattern of the wind on the water, but there are some that can fool anyone completely. In the first race of a Hornet World Championship at Plymouth, John Partridge and I were in the lead and sailing parallel to the breakwater about 150 yards inshore of it in an easterly direction on starboard tack. There was about a Force four breeze blowing and I was fully extended on the sliding seat. Suddenly, the boat came over on top of us. We quickly righted it and sailed on in the same direction on the opposite tack with me again right out on the end of the seat. You don't expect ninety degree shifts without warning in that weight of wind. Luckily we did not lose our lead, since Beecher Moore and his wife Bobbie who were behind us by seventy yards saw what happened. They eased both sheets, sat in the middle of their boat, and waited for the shift. When they got it we were upright and still seventy yards ahead. I'm glad to say that we went on to win that race, but I suffered so many traumatic experiences with the wind in Plymouth Sound that week that it almost put me off the place for life.

A perfectly sailed boat—note crew watching the water to windward for gusts while the skipper keeps his eyes on the sails. Again the fingertip grip is evident.

The discomfort of light weather when the crew has to support the sail to prevent the weight of the sheet from distorting its shape. Both crew and skipper are well forward, lifting the stern out to reduce wetted surface.

Most of the time on a beat the centreboard should be fully down. However, when the wind blows hard it must be raised to bring the centre of lateral resistance aft and balance the boat. Otherwise the skipper will have to apply a lot of weather helm and the rudder will act as a brake. Some helmsmen like the centreboard to point forward in very light weather to get a little extra feel, but this unbalances the boat.

In most winds the jib does not need tending on a windward leg except for the tack. When the wind has got very strong the crew may be required to free it in the knockdown puffs, and to sheet it in slowly again as soon as he can to provide the boat with the drive to keep going in the waves. In lightish airs the crew must have to ease the jib in lulls and pull it in in the puffs, but he must make sure that he does not over-sheet it in these conditions.

No crew should lose sight of the weather mark. He must not let the skipper overstand it. Often places are lost by rounding marks badly, so for those who round properly there is every chance of a gain. The approach will be made on starboard and the skipper will try to avoid tacking close to the mark, because this is where he can lose out when someone steams past to windward knocking all the wind out of the sails and possibly forcing him to tack twice more to get round.

9
The Close Reach

This is the leg that is omitted altogether from the Olympic course, but in club racing it occurs with great frequency. When it is blowing hard and boats are planing it is great fun; a little less wind and with marginal planing it is skilful; and in light weather it's a trifle boring, but nevertheless important. Some classes include a close reach in their championship courses, and because it can be exciting I think they are right to do so. By putting another wing mark on the opposite side of the Olympic course the reach between them is superb and the leg to the weather mark becomes a test of whether or not it can be laid without a tack. This extra triangle in the course is well worthwhile.

After the weather mark is rounded and the jib eased, the first job is to raise the centreboard. This may be quite difficult because of the heavy sideways pressures on the board, and is one of the few times that a raising-tackle led to each gunwale has value, particularly in the heavier going, because it allows the crew to stay sitting out. The centreboard has to come up to balance the boat by bringing the centre of lateral resistance aft, otherwise there would be a lot of weather helm. This causes the rudder to act as a brake and the boat becomes difficult to handle. The stronger the wind (greater pressure on the rig causes the centre of effort to move further aft), the higher the centreboard must be raised. Lining the inside of the centreboard slot with PTFE sheet will give you a centreboard that will move whatever the pressure on it. This is a job which can only be done when the boat is built or a new centreboard case put in, of course. PTFE (Teflon) is expensive, but any of the laminated plastics used for kitchen working surfaces makes a good substitute. However, PTFE should be used on the centreboard itself, the pieces required being relatively small.

The trim of the jib on a close reach is the real job of the crew and demands total concentration. Tell-tale wool yarns about eight inches from the luff of the jib make it easier. They help to show the wind flow across the sail and to indicate that the sail is not stalled on either side. By the time the sail itself lifts it has been stalled for some time, because modern sailcloths which are made of heat-set Dacron or Terylene are relatively stiff. There is no visible indication from the sail itself that it is over-sheeted, and this is the most important fault, but the tell-tales will show this. When the sail is perfectly set they will stream aft on both sides of the sail. When the jib is over-sheeted those on the weather side will tend to face forward or lift upwards. If the sail is eased too much, the leeward ones will drop. On a close reach the crew must keep his eyes glued to the tell-tales

Trimming the jib on a close reach means watching it like this and easing the sheet constantly in order to check that the sail is working at peak efficiency.

Close reaching, note how helmsman and crew have adopted a 'half out' position so that the crew is not in the most uncomfortable, just-over-the-side position, from which it is difficult to move either in or out.

and if they are both streaming aft he can be ninety per cent certain of doing his job well. There is still the boat to be kept upright—absolutely upright except in very light weather and smooth water when you help it to heel to leeward in order to reduce the wetted surface and sit forward to lift the stern clear to avoid drag.

When the wind increases sufficiently to allow marginal planing the crew will have his work cut out. This is the physical bit with a vengeance. In order to get the boat to rise onto a plane in the gusts the helmsman will luff slightly as the gust hits and pull the mainsheet in. The crew should trim the jib to match the main. Then as the boat starts to heel both skipper and crew sit out hard to slam the sails against the wind. At the same time they move their weight aft to lift the bow.

Spray flies as *Booth Holden*'s crew hold her upright on a close reach with the sheets just started. The two sheet men have to work in unison to get the best out of this eighteen footer under these conditions, and it's experience of regular sailing that tells.

Close reaching with a spinnaker, the American team of J. Brauch and D. Downing had the best speed of any of the 1973 World Championship boats in the 505s. This picture shows their technique. Weight well aft and pole well forward, the sheet is eased so that the spinnaker gives maximum forward drive and lift.

Luffing and slamming the boat upright and pulling the sheets increases the speed of the wind across the sails and encourages planing. As the boat gets up the helmsman will bear away, but the sheets do not need very much easing as the increased speed of the boat has brought the apparent wind further forward. Just as the boat is about to drop off the plane, the skipper will again luff to prolong planing as long as possible. When the plane is over the crew eases the jib sheets as the apparent wind comes aft; the helmsman will also bear away slightly and the crew will have to shift inboard. The jib tell-tales are still providing correct information on its trim. The crew's eyes should be peeled to weather for the sign of the coming gusts on the water: anticipation is the byword of a crew's success in these conditions.

As the wind gets stronger, planing becomes more prolonged until the point is reached when gusts that overpower the boat become the problem. Both helmsman and crew are sitting out as hard as they can, or the crew is fully extended on the trapeze with his weight aft, when one of these heavy gusts hits. The helmsman will ease the mainsheet and bear off to keep going flat out; the crew must ease the jib even beyond the stalling point to keep the boat upright. As soon as it begins to heel to leeward there is the danger of broaching, and it is possible to capsize. When this slam dies down the skipper will luff back to his original course and the crew will sheet the jib in to match the main. The tell-tales on the jib are just as useful when it's blowing hard as when it is light.

The importance of getting the boat to plane early and maintain that plane for as long as possible cannot be overstressed. Since boat speed is doubled by planing, the difference this can make is enormous. Whereas it is very hard to gain more than a few boat lengths on a beat to windward, it is easy to gain hundreds of yards on a reach by planing when rivals are not.

The close reach in a keelboat is not as rewarding as in a dinghy because they rarely plane. However, the principles which apply in a dinghy work in exactly the same way in a keelboat. Trimming the jib and the mainsail together will gain valuable seconds on this leg and may make the difference in gaining or breaking an overlap and getting a place further up the fleet.

10
Sitting-out

I can never think objectively of sitting-out without being reminded of the contribution made to this arduous part of sailing by Paul Elvstrom. He realized after his first Olympic regatta in 1948 that the weakest point of any of his rivals' sailing technique was in their inability to sit out continuously throughout the race. So he went home and trained until he could; but during this training he found out one or two major faults with gear and techniques and his cures for these have become standard practice in small boats today.

Formerly, toe straps in dinghies were fixed to the side of the centre-board trunk and crews were forced to sit out with their legs straight. Naturally enough this position is tiring, and being tiring it destroys concentration. While it is important to get the weight outboard as far as possible, it must be done so that the crew is comfortable. Therefore, it is of no use trying to sail a dinghy with one's knees outside the boat, because the strain of holding the body clear of the water is far too great to be able to maintain for very long: Elvstrom at the peak of his training found he could not manage it for more than six minutes and then he was so tired that his concentration was destroyed. Now toe straps are on the bottom of the dinghy and placed so that the knees come over the centre of the side deck. The gunwale presses on the backs of the thighs and the inside of the side deck on the top of the calf muscle. Foam rubber padding in the trousers helps take the discomfort out of these pressure points. In a reasonably fit state most people will find that they can stay in this position for a long time. Toe straps must be adjusted to suit the individual as comfort is at stake.

In the gusts it is possible to lean back from this position, taking the centre of gravity further outboard, but this is difficult to maintain for any length of time and it should be used only to keep the boat from heeling in the gusts. This flexibility will give any boat added speed.

Modern keelboat sitting-out is generally in the form of a 'mini-hike' developed in the Soling. I cannot understand how the style came to be called this as there is nothing 'mini' about it whatsoever. It involves the use of high toe straps so that the lower part of the legs from the knees to the ankles are along the side deck, the thighs go down the side of the boat, and the crew hangs there. Most Solings have handles for the crew to hang onto, so that they can alternate the strain between arms and stomach muscles and can use the handles to haul themselves inboard. However, I did notice a complete absence of these handles on Buddy Melge's gold medal winning Soling at Kiel in 1972. I asked his crew Bill Bentsen why, and he replied that

One crew doing all he can to get the boat upright in a gust. A little more mainsheet eased would produce more speed and less spectacle.

Close reaching in puffy winds—the crew in a slightly higher position than for going to windward so that he can move in over the gunwale in the lulls more easily.

they were painful to sit on if you went down in a hurry or got moved forward or aft by a wave. Painful to sit on by accident they might be, but unless you are Olympic fit I do recommend that you bolt them on for your own benefit. Now the Soling class allows the use of 'body belt' hiking aids used in conjunction with toe straps.

The more conventional keelboats such as Dragons do respond to being sat out by their crews. The old argument that the windage of the crew on the weather gunwale more than outweighed their righting moment has long been proved incorrect. It is difficult to sit out a boat where there are restrictions about toe straps being fitted in the right place, and so there is plenty of argument for lying along the weather side of the boat, gripping the gunwale with toes and fingers. It may be uncomfortable to begin with, but in time it can be found to be quite relaxing, however wet.

A wild ride on one of the few grey days in Sydney harbour for the three-man crew of KB. Here the forward man watches for wind and other boats; the middle man the sails, for he trims the mainsheet, and the skipper looks at the waves and feels his way to windward.

As the skipper bears off on the crest of each wave, the crew moves aft to lift the bow and encourage planing.

Trapezes are perhaps the most exciting and efficient way of using crew weight to advantage. In the next chapter Colin Turner deals with the techniques of the trapeze and I propounded my thoughts on the type of harness you should use in Chapter V. The gear must be properly arranged for crew to be fully efficient. It is little use, for instance, having the return elastic take the trapeze wire back so that it lies adjacent to the shroud. When the crew grabs for the handle as he tacks, he is bound to catch hold of the shroud as well at least eighty per cent of the time. It is best to separate the shroud and trapeze wire by six inches at least. Besides having a double ring giving height adjustment, there must be a jamming block in the system which allows you to adjust more finely the height you want for the particular weather conditions. The flatter the sea the lower the crew can go; but he must be higher in waves or he will stop the boat as he hits them.

For the wire itself, $\frac{5}{32}$ inch diameter 1×19 stainless steel is ideal. It has a 1000 pound breaking strain which should be enough for the worse shock loads it has to encounter when the boat is bouncing off the tops of big waves and dropping into the troughs. The wires do get kinked from time to time, and should be checked for possible fracture frequently. Crews look very stupid if the wire or any of the adjusting line breaks. I well know: it happened to me on the way out to the start of the second race of the Little America's Cup in 1967. I had lengthened the whole system with a short rope grommet between the bottom adjusting block and the ring the previous afternoon. I had made this of polypropylene rope and worked it round as one long splice and then sealed the six strand ends with a match. Polypropylene rope has a low melting point, and I had melted most of the strands and they became brittle. One small wave was enough to put on the shock load that broke it. We had time to go ashore and effect the necessary repair before the start: if not, my 'Beecher pack' would have been put to use early on.

The attachment on the harness is again a matter of preference. In the early days I was all for the gate-latch type, particularly after I had made mine stand out reasonably rigidly from the belt. It was very positive and I had to make a deliberate effort to disengage it. But it was cumbersome, and after a time I changed to an open hook. Later this was improved with a nylon spring latch at the mouth, but I am now doubtful whether this is necessary. Thick elastic for the trapeze return is not efficient; it is better to use the thinnest possible and take its run for a long distance so that the pull on the ring is very light and does not in any way affect the crew when fully extended.

The type of handle is a question of personal preference. For many years I preferred the triangular one made of stainless steel, but there are now some plastic handles on the market which thread onto the trapeze wire. These are fine, provided that there is some tape around the wire to prevent cutting between the index and middle fingers.

Sliding seats are not common, but after all the years I have been using one it would not be right to leave them out. I think they are the greatest thing since sliced bread, but I am biased. Certainly they are one of the easiest means of sitting out. The Hornet rules allow the seat to project three feet and three inches beyond the gunwale, which gives the person with an average leg length a comfortable stretch to the end of the seat, but for most that is not enough in a breeze. It is easy to work one's backside over the end of the seat and tuck the toes underneath. This puts the crew about a foot further out than the trapeze man.

Tacking with a seat is simple: it is a case of sliding in, lifting the aft leg over the seat, and facing forward. As the crew goes for the new jib sheet with one hand he slides the seat across by its strap with the other and then climbs out. It is faster than a trapeze, with full control of the jib at the same time.

Spinnaker trimming from the end of the seat is a delight, as many crews of Australian Skates and VJs will know. It was the Australians who put a new light on sliding seats in the Hornet class: instead of using one which runs in a tray, which prevents its movement fore and aft, they introduced a seat anchored at both gunwales in loops which allow a certain amount of pivot. This fore and aft movement has brought the seat back into full contention with the trapeze.

One sitting-out aid which never got a great deal of publicity was the small wooden handles which hinged up from the thwart and came six inches or so above the gunwale of an International 14. They were known as 'ladies' aids' and used much like the grab handles on a Soling. Since the introduction of trapezes into the class they have all disappeared.

Having just rounded the weather mark, the crew has moved aft to get the boat planing at maximum speed as the skipper bears away on to the correct course. Then the spinnaker will go up.

11
Trapezing Techniques
by Colin Turner

Trapezing in its present form was developed during the IYRU two-man centreboard trials which saw the introduction of such classes as the Flying Dutchman, Coronet (the forerunner of the 505) and Osprey which spread rapidly throughout the yachting world. There were three trials to select a new class for international racing. At the second, in September 1952, the Osprey sailed by John Oakeley and Cliff Norbury appeared with a trapeze wire supporting the crew at waist level. The development of this equipment was not without its humorous side. The system consisted of a hook on the wire and a ring on the harness. Unfortunately, the designer Ian Proctor made a serious miscalculation: the hook he recommended was a modified butcher's hook. Ian's assumption that Cliff Norbury weighed less than a side of beef was proved incorrect when the hook straightened and deposited Cliff into the water. In the final trials, which resulted in the selection of the Flying Dutchman, nearly all of the competitors used a trapeze. An earlier form of the trapeze was used by Beecher Moore in his Thames A Rater, the crew hanging on to the 'bell rope' with his hands. In 1938 Peter Scott used a trapeze on his International 14 *Thunder and Lightning*, in this case with a belt at chest level. Not only did he succeed in winning the coveted Prince of Wales Cup using this new-fangled device, but caused the class to ban this sitting-out aid. It has taken many years for the International 14s to realize the merits of the trapeze, but its recent adoption has injected a new life into the class. Four of the six Olympic classes selected for the 1976 Olympics use trapezes, indicating that the technique is accepted as an efficient method of sitting out.

Trapezing technique can be summed up in one word—balance. Strength, although an asset, is not essential, allowing girls to compete on even terms with the traditional 'hairy gorillas'. This fact on its own must justify the uses of the trapeze. The crew should be suspended from a point just above the body's centre of gravity. Attachment too high increases the effort required to stay out flat on the wire and makes it harder to get off the wire. Attachment too low can cause spectacular if unwanted departure of crew from boat. When suspended from the correct point it is possible to spring a couple of feet clear of the gunwale and return gently to rest on the balls of the feet. The position of the feet and the attitude

The perfect trapeze position, the whole body balanced around the hook and little pressure on the balls of the crew's feet. (*Guy Gurney*)

of the legs are important. If the feet are placed too close together it will be very difficult to retain balance even against normal movement. With the feet placed too far apart the crew becomes rigidly attached to the boat, unable to move with it. The feet should be placed about one and a half feet apart, the legs being slightly bent and the weight taken on the balls of the feet. This stance allows the crew to move with the motion of the boat and alter his fore and aft position easily.

It is very noticeable that once a crew has decided on the correct fore and aft trim for a given leg they concentrate on athwartship trim only. In certain conditions small boats respond to constant adjustment to fore and aft trim. This was effectively demonstrated to me by a former Fireball World Champion, Peter Bateman. Sailing to windward in a chop, the bow was lifted clear of a wave by moving one and a half feet aft, returning forward as the boat reached the top of the wave. Other boats in this race were stopping as they hit each wave, and we arrived at the windward mark with a comfortable lead. This weight adjustment would have been difficult when using toe straps or a sliding seat.

The crew in the boat on the left has gone without hooking on the trapeze—his entire weight is supported by one arm. The sudden gust as they tacked had to be counteracted, but the skipper must ease the mainsheet or the Japanese boat will tack inside and get round the buoy clear ahead.

By allowing the boat to heel to leeward and then bringing it upright rapidly (easy using a wire, difficult when using toe straps), it can be moved directly to windward. This technique, which requires practice to co-ordinate crew and helmsman, can be used to good effect when overtaking to windward and wishing to clear the wind shadow of a boat dead ahead without having to tack.

A number of trapeze artists think that it is necessary to keep their weight as low as possible. This does not always give the maximum righting movement, and the correct height is at gunwale level. Except in heavy conditions, trapezing with the spinnaker set requires the crew to be mobile rather than to exert maximum righting moment. The trapeze should be adjustable or have an additional ring so that the crew can sit over the side, supported by the wire, as if using toe straps. From this position it is possible to 'walk' in and out of the boat, leaving both hands free to trim the sheets. Being able to trapeze at this height is also useful when sailing in gusty conditions which only require the crew's weight on the wire in the puffs, speed when going out and coming in on the wire being more important than maximum righting moment. A Fireball allowed to come beyond upright and heel to windward when sailing falls off rapidly to leeward. It takes a long time to recover the ground lost by allowing the boat to come past upright because you could not reduce you righting moment rapidly. When trapezing low, the crew must watch not only the trim of the boat but also the waves. It is not desirable for the crew to pass through the waves; not only does he get wet, but it also stops the boat.

The crew should lift himself clear of the waves, not by using the handle, which pulls the boat on top of him, but by bending his knees. This rapidly brings his centre of gravity towards the boat, allowing it to heel to leeward lifting him above the wave. The helmsman can also help by steering the boat over rather than through waves. Certain boats do have to be driven through the waves, however, in which case the crew should not trapeze too low.

So far in this chapter I have dealt with the action of the crew on the wire. The biggest obstacle to the beginners is often getting on and off the wire. One can, of course, get out holding onto the trapeze handle, hooking on when you are out on the wire. This requires two hands and the jib therefore has to be cleated before the crew 'leaves' the boat. This technique can lead to problems: it requires practice and fitness.

The traditional method can be thought of as five separate actions. The key to its successful execution is that the crew sits over the side. When the trapeze wire becomes tight between the mast and the harness it is a simple matter to move out over the gunwale into the extended trapezing position.

1 The crew sits on the side of the dinghy, clipping the trapeze ring to the harness using the forward arm. The hand is then run along the trapeze system to the handle, keeping tension on the lower part of the trapeze system.
2 The hand is then swung out over the shoulder until the wire becomes tight between the handle and the mast.
3 Keeping tension on this arm one eases out backwards into a position similar to that adopted when using toe straps.
4 The forward foot is brought up to the gunwale.
5 The forward leg is then straightened, and the aft foot brought onto the gunwale.

In moderate winds sitting out for the crew is aided by the trapeze, here hooked onto the higher of the two rings. Barry Dunning is just about to move his forward foot onto the gunwale and flatten this Fireball against the wind to drive through the choppy sea.

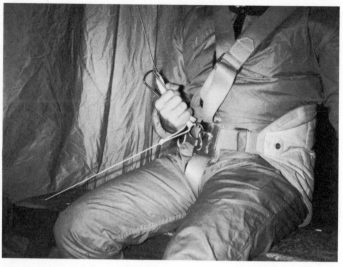

a.

Sequence of Colin Turner showing correct trapeze technique for going out.
a.   A firm grip on the double ring on the wire at the moment of hooking on.
b.   Out over the side with the weight of the body on the wire.

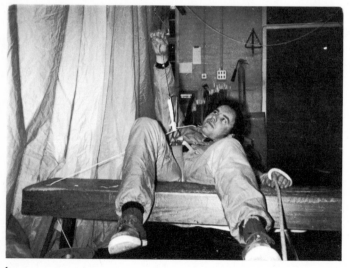

b.

c.

c. d. e. Forward foot on gunwale, hand on handle to remove any slack in the wire.

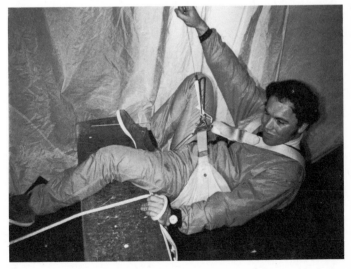

d.

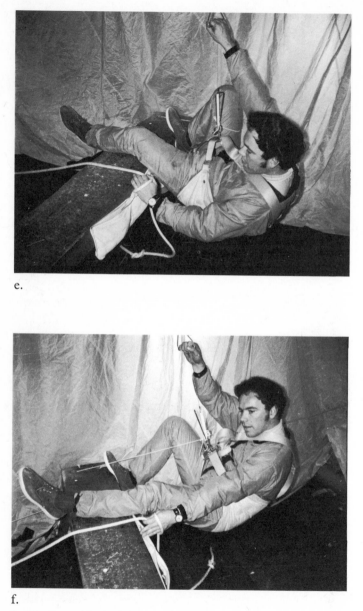

e.

f.

f. The forward leg begins to stretch until . . .

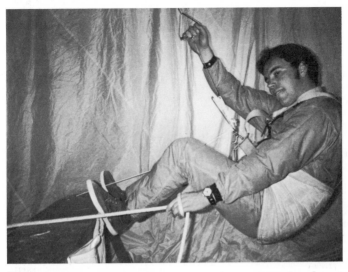

g.

g. The aft foot comes up to the gunwale.

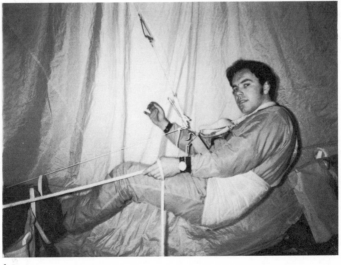

h.

h. i. The legs are straightened.

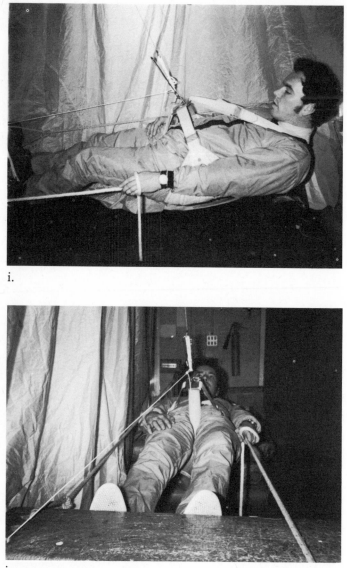

i.

j.

j.   The perfect trapezing position with the balls of the feet on the gunwale and the feet just far enough apart to balance the body.

One often hears crews saying they can tack from wire to wire in so many seconds. The time might seem impressive, and when practicing tacking in a Tempest we could reduce this time to about eight seconds. This quick tack, however, stopped the boat dead. A slower, smoother tack of twelve seconds was found to be more efficient, the boat retaining maximum possible speed at all points of the manoeuvre. It is important when tacking to make the action a smooth flowing one.

Positioning the jib sheets plays an important part in this manoeuvre. They should be led from a point aft of the normal trapezing position. Jammers for the sheets should also be very carefully positioned; it is essential that the sheets can be released easily while the crew is extended on the wire.

Steering from a wire is probably one of the most exciting sensations of sailing. It calls for a slightly different technique—an extra arm would also be useful. It always pay to trapeze at a height which enables you to get back in easily. One problem when sailing singlehanded on a Unicorn catamaran, for example, is that on a reach it is necessary to be as far aft as possible. The angle of the trapeze wire tends to pull the crew forward at the slightest provocation. Carefully positioned toe straps on the gunwale are of great assistance. The tendency is to pivot about the forward foot, with the after foot leaving the gunwale. Equilibrium can be restored by dragging the rear foot in the water; this will stop you swinging forward, slowing the boat down and allowing you to regain some semblance of control.

Constant checking of the trapeze gear is essential. Going over the fittings at one World Championship, I found both sets of lanyards chafed through. If this had not been spotted I would not only have got very wet, but we could have also lost a World Championship. It is said that familiarity breeds contempt: having used a trapeze belt for three seasons I failed to examine it before another World Championship series. The hook broke during the fourth race because of a weld failure. My involuntary swim caused us to lose places which proved critical in the final total.

It is important to relax when trapezing, conserving energy for the strenuous parts of sailing. Trapezing allows the crew to take a more active part in the race: quite often the man on the wire is the only one who has a clear view of what is happening, the helmsman being immersed in spray. Of course the crew will get the blame for going the wrong way, and little praise will be given if the correct course has been indicated. But it is a team effort and one to which the crew out on the wire can contribute greatly. You have to know what is going on and why the skipper wants to do it to be really helpful, so ask him why he does things—when you get ashore. When you are aware of the problems you are better qualified to cure them. From the trapeze you have the best view: use your advantage fully.

A lot of things wrong which the crew could help to put right. The lady skipper has got a lot of weather helm, which could be decreased by easing the spinnaker sheet until the luff just begins to lift. The main boom end is in the water and easing the kicking strap will help by allowing the boom end to raise, spilling wind from the leech well up, thereby reducing the heel. The jib is not sheeted and the crew are not sitting out this Soling properly.

12
The Broad Reach, the Run and the Gybe

As soon as the wind comes aft of the beam the crew is more in charge, or he is on all boats that set a spinnaker. There is very little fun or skill needed in sailing downwind legs without a spinnaker. Only when it is blowing really hard can the spinnakerless crew derive any satisfaction from these legs.

Coming onto a downwind leg, the most important thing for the crew to do after easing the jib is to raise the centreboard. In anything of a breeze the skipper is going to find it difficult to control the boat with the rudder if the plate is not well up.

Lateral balance is now more important. Bad movement in the boat, now that the crew is not solely concerned in holding it upright against the force of the wind, can cause wild rolling and a subsequent dip in the water. Catlike movement is now imperative. Crew and skipper will have to work together to create balance, and to improve this balance there is no substitute for sailing hours.

If there is any chance that the spinnaker will set it must go up. (Barry Dunning deals with this procedure in the next chapter.) Skippers should never panic their crews by shouting at this stage; a routine, followed systematically, is all-important. If it goes wrong time after time, the routine needs examining because the foul-ups would seem to stem from there.

Once the spinnaker is up, to trim it the crew must be able to see it and that means that he should sit to windward. There are some old fashioned helmsmen who don't like sitting to leeward or doing the balancing on the downwind legs, but they have to train themselves to do it. The crew must concentrate totally on getting every available ounce of power from the spinnaker and to do this he needs assistance from the back of the boat.

The spinnaker is not just a bag to trap wind. It works like the other two sails, by utilizing a flow of air across from luff to luff. If it is oversheeted it will stop the boat, and if it is undersheeted it will stall and flap. Getting the sheeting right comes with experience and experience comes with practice. The elements of trimming a spinnaker boil down to keeping the two clews level, the pole as far aft as it will come in relation to the wind, and easing the sheet until the weather luff begins to lift. To do this well needs concentration of the highest order. All the time the weather luff of the spinnaker should be kept just on the stall point, as in this way the crew will not over-sheet the sail. He must try to get the pole aft all the time, but also be prepared to ease it forward again if the sail won't set with the pole aft. The burgee or wind indicator will give the best guide to where the pole should be: the pole set at right angles to the flag is a good basis to work from.

Never for one second can the crew take his eyes off the spinnaker or it is bound to collapse. He must not worry that he is coming to the end of the leg and that the spinnaker has got to come down—it is the helmsman's responsibility to tell him when to get it down, the crew's to keep it going while it's up.

If the leg is too shy for the spinnaker to be set efficiently, the crew must tell the skipper. He will then decide whether to fall off to leeward of the course to keep it going or whether to drop it instantly. There are times when it is set and not doing the slightest good: particularly when it is set with the sheet hard in and backwinding the mainsail. Then the kite is only pushing the boat sideways. All those little force arrows on the theoretical diagrams of sailing are acting to heel the boat and there is no resultant forward component producing drive. That is the time to get it down. This is one time the crew can cheat his man at the back. If he is absolutely certain that the spinnaker is doing more harm than good, he should let it flap wildly and shout 'won't set' or words to that effect. The skipper will call for it down in a brace of shakes.

In light or moderate conditions there are few problems for the crew. Once he is in a comfortable position for the leg, and this may be fully extended on the trapeze, he should stay there and let the helmsman deal with the boat's balance. It is when the wind gets stronger that the fun begins. When planing starts, the need for greater awareness comes with it. To get the best out of the boat the skipper is going to use the waves and gusts together. He will endeavour to use the gusts to bear off down the face of the waves, and as he bears off the crew should ease the spinnaker sheet but be ready to re-sheet it as the boat accelerates and the apparent wind comes forward. As the lull comes he will luff, and the crew must only draw in the sheet as much as is necessary to prevent the spinnaker collapsing. With skill, the skipper is aiming to collect the next gust as he climbs to the crest of the next wave to surge forward as before. The crew can help to promote the plane by pulling equally on the guy and sheet just before the boat starts to go down the face of the wave. This needs lots of practice in order to get the timing just right or else it is wasted.

Generally, the harder it blows and the broader the reach the farther aft the crew will go in the boat. In light air the crew should be well forward to lift the stern and cut down the wetted area, but as planing begins the bow must be encouraged to rise and that means the crew moves aft. In waves the crew will have to 'ooch' in addition to playing the sheets, by moving forward and aft in sympathy with the waves, leaning forward as the boat climbs up the backs and coming aft with a deliberate movement as it breaks the crest and starts the wild run down the face. The crew then holds his place until the boat has gone through the trough and started to

There's a fascination for the bottom of this boat. Crew's eyes should never leave the spinnaker and perhaps the skipper might feel more comfortable out of his wetsuit on a hot airless day like this.

climb up the back of the next one. It pays to help when breaking the crest of the wave to tip the boat forwards, the helmsman and crew jerking their bodies forward just at the crucial moment.

The broader the reach the more unstable the boat becomes; it is most unstable on a dead run. More care is needed in balancing the boat, the further aft the wind comes. Since it rarely pays to run directly before the wind—only in dead light airs is it effective—the running leg should be sailed in two very broad reaches with a gybe in the middle.

Gybing should not be feared; instead it should be practised. When it is blowing hard helmsman and crew should go out and practise gybe after gybe until they have mastered the technique. There are times when it is necessary to gybe in a hurry—manoeuvring before the start or at the wing mark when in a pack of boats—and to funk it would be disastrous. So confidence in gybing is all-important at both ends of the boat.

Gybing in light to moderate airs should present the crew with little problem apart from maintaining the balance of the boat. As the wind increases he will encounter certain problems apart from keeping the spinnaker trimmed. He must always make sure that the jib is uncleated and cannot fill after the gybe on the wrong side. He may be asked to help the boom across. When he is, he should pull hard when he gets the command and be sure to duck as the boom comes across. For the helmsman's sake the crew must not over-correct with his weight or the double correction will cause a bad roll and consequent loss of forward motion.

When running in very strong winds it pays to have the spinnaker guy and sheet well forward of the normal position. This stops the spinnaker from rolling from side to side and setting up a 'death wobble'. The gunwale hooks that are used for the guy are ideal for this purpose. To help balance the boat in the stronger breezes the crew must be aware of the forces that the spinnaker develops. Because of its curved section it provides side forces as well as those at right angles to its chord base, and therefore by pulling on the sheet or guy the crew can affect the heel. If the boat heels to windward he should pull on the sheets and it will come upright; if it heels to leeward he pulls on the guy.

Approaching the leeward mark, the sequence of events in the boat should be such that those things which least affect speed are done first. The mast is re-raked and the sail controls are set up for the beat. Then the spinnaker is dropped and packed away, and finally as the boat is about to round the buoy the crew lowers the centreboard. The jib and mainsail should then come in together, maintaining the right angle to the wind at all times. That also takes a lot of practice, but done properly it can gain valuable seconds.

Since this is the point of sailing on which crews can contribute most to the boat's success, they should get all the practice that they can. The words 'gybe' and 'spinnaker' have been known to instil fear into some crews, and I suppose they still do, but there should be no reason for it. These are fun legs to sail, and by having confidence in himself the crew can make a great deal of difference to the boat's performance.

The hoisting order is going to be right on this American Fireball. The crew will have the pole in position as the mark is rounded and then the spinnaker can go up.

And this, at 800 ft or so, is not the biggest spinnaker of this 18 ft skiff, but it will need the full co-ordination of the four-man crew to keep it drawing perfectly like this.

13
Spinnaker Handling in Dinghies
Part I - Hoisting, Setting and Lowering
by Barry Dunning

Nowadays more and more races are being won downwind with the spinnaker and with perfection in teamwork, than upwind. The art of downwind sailing is not something which can be picked up easily, but it is something which must be practised and practised again, to get it right.

We all have our own ideas about spinnaker drills and they differ from class to class, but they can be grouped under two broad headings: a system where the crew is using a trapeze, and one where the crew is leaning out with toe straps. Each of these must be further categorized as to the boats that have spinnaker chutes, and the others with bins by the side of or in front of the mast.

One of the biggest problems in a spinnaker system is friction and the halyards and mast must be examined to see if any of this can be alleviated. The most obvious place is at the sheaves in the foot of the mast and at the hounds where the normal dinghy spinnaker halyard comes out. Most manufacturers usually run the spinnaker halyard through the groove where the mainsail luff rope and the main and jib halyards run, but I have found it best to move the halyard from this groove to the inside of the mast tube. I put a sheave at the hounds and another at the bottom of the tube. This gets rid of any foul-ups between the spinnaker halyard and the jib and main halyards, an improvement necessary not only with a spinnaker chute, but with any system. Next check the spinnaker chute system where the halyard comes from the sheave to the skipper's hand, look for any spots where friction could occur; over knees, around pulleys and through fairleads. It is important that the cleat for the sheet is properly sited, either close to the fairlead or on the side deck on the opposite side of the boat. There are various ways of cleating the spinnaker sheet and guy, some illustrated here. Another important factor is the positioning of the spinnaker guy. The last thing a crew wants is the guy running across his back when he is sitting on the side deck, or across the trapeze wire; instead a gunwale hook is used. The gunwale hook has various forms: manufactured ones resemble metal hooks with rubber grommets in them, or they can be as simple as those used in Flying Dutchmen which are nothing more than a groove cut in the gunwale. The gunwale groove has the advantage that when the boat is gybed, the guy (which is then the sheet) comes out of the groove very easily, whereas with the metal hook it has to be taken out, and this takes time.

Another improvement that can be made is to taper the sheets. One-eighth inch diameter Terylene rope is plenty strong enough to take the strain of the spinnakers, but it is almost impossible to cleat, and very, very painful to hold. Quarter inch diameter rope cleats well and is pleasant to hold. The outer casing of a plaited quarter inch rope is pulled back over the core for about a foot and nine inches are cut off the core. The eighth inch rope is sewn to the end of the core and the outer casing of the quarter inch rope carefully pulled over the eighth inch until it lays properly. Then by sewing through the outer casing and the eighth inch rope for the length of the splice the whole thing becomes firm. To finish, a light whipping is put on each end of this splice with fine waxed thread. The sheet will then run easier through the spinnaker pole and it has the added advantage that the weight of the sheets is reduced on the spinnaker, allowing it to set more satisfactorily in light weather.

The spinnaker halyard should be tapered when a chute system is used, at least where the end of the halyard is attached to the reinforcing patch on the spinnaker. This also makes the spinnaker easier to set in light weather. The best stuff to use is a very, very light polypropylene cord. Before 1969 in the Merlin Rocket class we used to always hoist the spinnaker on the side or in front of the mast without the aid of a spinnaker chute and it was with this system that we perfected a modification on a Clamcleat (Page 100). It entailed a little work with a file and a hacksaw, but made a cleat that was very useful for keeping the spinnaker halyard in place. This cleat used to be on the side deck next to the spinnaker basket. I also used to put a knot in the spinnaker halyard about nine inches away from the head of the spinnaker so that I could not pull the spinnaker right to the top. Make certain that the knot is not too small or it can be pulled into the sheaves at the hounds, and the spinnaker will then not come down. A wide, light washer on the halyard above the knot will stop this happening.

The spinnaker pole and its topping lift/downhaul system are most important. I have always gone for simplicity and find the most successful is the plastic fork system, using a series of knots on the uphaul which allow variation in the height of the spinnaker pole (below). In another system there is a cleat at the bottom of the mast so that the pole height can be altered. It has the disadvantage that the pole moves because the slack has to

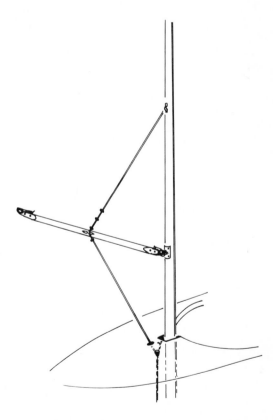

The simple spinnaker boom vang system with knots on the rope to vary the pole height and a shockcord on a lazy pulley under the deck to keep it out of the way when not in use.

be taken up by elastic, whereas with the knots the pole is very rigid. If the bottom of the downhaul is attached about nine inches in front of the mast, there is a pull forward on the pole, taking it onto the spinnaker, which saves having to push the pole forward when the guy is pulled aft. Paul Davies (see Part Two) does not agree with me, but I find this best for small dinghies. The problems of handling the smaller spinnakers are slightly different to those on Flying Dutchmen, 505s and Fireballs, simply because of the lower strains involved.

The trip string on the pole for the end fittings can take various forms. The most usual is a continuous string from one end fitting to the other, but the experience of top crews questions the practicality of this system since invariably if one end is pulled the other end is also released. This can be corrected by lashing the trip string in the centre. A refinement of this is a system with a sleeve or handle that goes over the spinnaker pole, made of soft plastic tube to which the trip strings are attached. If you pull the handle one way it keeps the string slack at the other end and does not pull that fitting open (below). This works very well. If it saves just a few seconds each time the spinnaker is used during the race, this can add up to a few boat lengths, and that is all races are won by.

The Barry Dunning refinement to the spinnaker boom with plastic tube sleeves to which the pole end trip strings are attached.

There is much less use of the bag or basket stowed spinnaker since the introduction of launcher chutes. There are two ways of hoisting depending on who pulls the halyard. The helmsman normally pulls the sail up on a more stable boat like the Tempest or the 470, whereas in a fairly tender boat like the Merlin Rocket or the Lark it is normal for the crew to pull the spinnaker up. This is still so with the advent of spinnaker chutes, but a change is likely as more skippers begin to see the common sense of pulling the halyard themselves.

A spinnaker hoist with the halyard led aft to the helmsman is best described in two separate parts—helmsman and crew. The crew picks up the pole from the bottom of the boat and starts attaching the guy. The helmsman then hoists the spinnaker, and when it is up he trims the sheet, balancing the boat meanwhile. As the helmsman is hoisting, the crew is making sure that the sheets are free after he has clipped the pole onto the guy, and then attaches the uphaul/downhaul and clips the pole onto the mast. He then pulls the guy, bringing the weather clew of the spinnaker up to the pole. The crew can sit either to windward or to leeward, depending on the conditions; normally, it is to leeward in very light weather and to windward in every other set of conditions. In a system where the crew hoists the spinnaker, the helmsman pulls the pole out from the bottom of the boat and hands it to the crew when the spinnaker is hoisted, balancing the boat and trimming the sheet and guy. The halyard should come out of the mast at about waist height, going straight through a cam jam cleat. The crew then pulls the rest of the guy round the forestay from the leeward side until the clew of the spinnaker is in sight and cleats it. He then clips the spinnaker pole to the guy, attaches the uphaul/downhaul and clips the pole onto the mast. In the meantime the helmsman should have got the spinnaker drawing. The crew then sits to weather or to leeward, whichever is easier for him to have sight of the spinnaker, and he is then in control on downwind legs. The second system obviously takes longer, and is included here for academic interest.

Hoisting a spinnaker with a launcher chute, the skipper should pull the halyard. As the helmsman bears off round the mark, the crew pulls the pole from the bottom of the boat, clips on the loose guy which runs through the spinnaker pole end, attaches the pole to the uphaul/downhaul system and hooks the pole onto the mast. He then pulls the sheet to help the spinnaker out of the chute and also tries to pull the guy at the same time, making sure that the guy is underneath the gunwale hook. In the meantime the helmsman is pulling the spinnaker out of the chute with the halyard, making sure the retrieving line does not get fouled up in the sock of the chute.

A lot of places are won and sailing downwind when taking the spinnaker down. Vital seconds can be saved if the system is a good one and if things are done smoothly and correctly. Without a spinnaker chute the order is: the crew comes in, easing the sheet as he does so, unclips the spinnaker pole from the mast and pulls the guy towards him, detaching the downhaul in the process. He then unclips the pole from the guy and stows the pole, putting it into the bottom of the boat. He then pulls the weather clew of the spinnaker towards him and gathers in the foot (about two-thirds is sufficient). He then calls to the skipper to let go the halyard and stows it as quickly and as tidily as he can in the spinnaker basket. If he has the halyard clear on the mast in front of him he does not have to ask the helmsman to let go, but he should let him know what he is doing. Meanwhile, the helmsman is making sure that the sheet and the guy are tidy and not trailing in the water.

With a spinnaker chute the order is different. The helmsman lets the halyard go and pulls in on the retrieving line. The crew, in the meantime, lets the spinnaker sheet go, but not the guy—this is still held, thus supporting the spinnaker and stopping it going underneath the boat. As the spinnaker starts to go tight in the chute he lets the guy go, comes in, takes the pole off the mast, disconnects the downhaul and stows it in the bottom of the boat. The crew then goes out on his wire or leans flat out and leaves the tidying up to the helmsman or until sufficient time is available that he can do it himself.

The primary consideration when flying a spinnaker is that it only gets dynamic lift when there is air flowing across it: therefore a spinnaker is not used to stop the wind, but to get flow across it. This is one of the main reasons why when trimming a spinnaker the point to watch is the windward luff, and it must be trimmed so that the luff is just on the point of lifting, much like sailing with a jib. It is also one of the reasons why it pays to tack downwind rather than to run dead before the breeze. On a dead run, it is very easy for the sail to be over-sheeted and so lose drive. It is important always to watch the angle of the spinnaker pole to the wind; it invariably pays to keep it at about ninety degrees to the wind.

The height of the spinnaker pole, or more truly the outboard end, is critical. There are various rules of thumb, and various styles in different classes in the way it is set. Basically, the clews of the spinnaker should be kept at the same height. It pays to carry the spinnaker pole lower when the breeze is light and a little higher in the heavier winds, allowing the weather clew to match the leeward (free) one. This, of course, is not true of all spinnakers, but is a good general rule, and never far out. There are three things to watch: the height and angle of the spinnaker pole, the luff that is to windward, and the burgee to make sure that the spinnaker is not over-sheeted.

Many people put the pole on the wrong way up. The draw pins must be facing upwards, so that when releasing the spinnaker pole from the guy, the pole drops away from it. It also makes it far easier to remove the pole from the mast when the pole, for some reason, rises up in the air.

When to furl the genoa or the jib is always a problem. Invariably it pays to have the jib furled on a dead run when the spinnaker is being used, because the jib is normally just flapping uselessly behind the mainsail. However, on a reach, depending on how fast the boat is and at what angle it is going, it seems to pay to keep the jib unfurled. However, this is not true in very light weather when reaching, when it sometimes pays to furl the jib and let the air flow around the spinnaker unhindered.

A good gybe is one in which the spinnaker does not collapse and the boat does not lose forward momentum. Invariably this means that the helmsman must steer the boat round and not

At the leeward mark all should be stowed in time to round the buoy properly. This crew has got it almost right, but a little tweak on the starboard spinnaker sheet would stop it trailing in the water.

slam it round the mark. It is easy to see that when a boat turns round a gybe mark very sharply it not only loses speed, but ends up with the spinnaker flapping in the breeze, thus giving no forward drive at all. There are various methods of gybing, but the basic rules are the same. The helmsman bears away from a close reach onto a dead run; the crew pulls back on the guy bringing the pole square with the wind and then cleats the guy and the sheet. The helmsman gybes the mainsail and as the boom comes over the crew resheets the jib. Then the crew takes the pole from the mast, clips it onto the new guy, moves the downhaul across, unhitches the sheet from the pole and then clips the pole onto the mast.

The system I use, however, is slightly different in that I square the spinnaker pole up, then cleat the sheet and guy, and then detach the pole completely from the mast, guy and downhaul and move it into the centre of the boat, the spinnaker still filling, but flying unattached. The helmsman then gybes the mainsail while in the meantime I clip the pole onto the new guy and push it out to weather. This moves the spinnaker across the boat smoothly without collapsing it. I then clip on the downhaul system and clip the pole onto the mast. This takes a lot of practice, and does provide the crew the chance to lose the pole overboard in the middle of the gybe. I would recommend, therefore, not to attempt it until full confidence in the previous system has been achieved.

On an Olympic course the gybe is between two fairly close reaches, and so to gybe the boat must first be put onto a dead run to get the pole across. Then the crew can let it go forward and pull in on the spinnaker sheet as the helmsman luffs onto the new course.

There is no substitute for practice in gybing. It is a complicated manoeuvre and can only be perfected by practice. The points to remember always when setting a spinnaker are:

1 Keep the clews level; this means that the spinnaker is set correctly.

2 If the wind is lighter, the pole must come down because the leeward clew will not be supported by the wind.

3 Keep the flow across the sail.

4 In the heavier winds, if the clew is low the luff of the spinnaker is strangling the flow of air across it. By easing the pole up, the luff of the spinnaker is freed.

Look at the boat, look at the fittings, look at the mast, look at the shape of the spinnaker. If the pole is at the right height, there are light tapered sheets, the spinnaker chute has a friction-free system, then nothing stands in the crew's way. With a really efficient boat all that is needed is practice, practice and more practice—there is no substitute, and invariably those who win are the ones who not only put more effort into the boat, but just put in more time.

Gybing technique being demonstrated well by Frank Davis and Stuart Kelday. Davis, the skipper, has pulled the helm up and is grabbing the mainsheet to pull the boom over while Kelday squares the spinnaker into approximately the right position for the next leg. Ideally the kite should not stop drawing.

Shows the piece of a standard Clam cleat cut away to keep spinnaker halyard in place when not using a launcher chute.

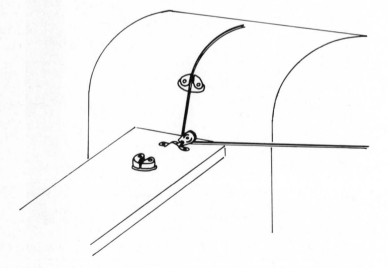

The spinnaker sheet of a 470 goes through a lazy pulley mounted on the centre thwart. When used as a guy it is cleated in the jammer mounted on the side tank and when necessary as a sheet, in the cleat mounted on a block on the thwart.

Part II~Gear is the limiting factor: some ways of improving it
by Paul Davies

Hard luck stories of ifs and buts heard at the club bar after races usually relate to experiences on the windward legs of the course. Poor downwind performance always seems to be put down to failings in the boat, and very few helmsmen and crew will admit or even realize that their inferior speed off the wind is invariably due to lack of preparation and lack of teamwork.

I will deal with teamwork first, and then discuss preparation and how it can assist the efficient handling of the boat downwind. Let us assume that the boat is approaching the windward mark in the middle of the fleet and that the leading boats have settled down on the next leg of the course. While the helmsman is concentrating on approaching and rounding the mark, the crew should use every spare moment to observe the leading boats and prepare for hoisting the spinnaker if it can be set.

The crew should tell the helmsman the position of the next mark, whether the leaders are on course or sailing high or low, what the tide is doing, and if there will be clear wind when round the mark. If not, whether he should reach high under two sails and then pop the spinnaker or whether it would pay to hoist the spinnaker quickly and go to leeward. It usually pays to go high in planing conditions and straight or low in light winds. Helmsman and crew must decide before rounding the mark what the plan is; it is hopeless having the crew coming in ready to hoist the spinnaker if the helmsman intends doing a quick squirt up to weather first.

Everything must be ready in the boat for a fast spinnaker hoist. The pole should be on the correct side and easily accessible. The crew should look around the boat to make sure everything is ready; if he is flat out on the trapeze there is not much that can be done (hence the need for perfect pre-race preparation), but if it is light weather the crew can sneak the spinnaker pole onto the guy before rounding the mark. Some Flying Dutchmen and other dinghies can carry the pole on the foredeck already hooked on, but this will only be useful for the first hoist as the crew will, in all probability, have stowed the pole in the bottom of the boat during the rush into the leeward mark.

Once the decision has been made to go for the spinnaker it must be up as quickly as possible. This might sound very basic, but how often do you see a really slick well-practiced hoist? If it is light or you are on a broad reach or a dead run, the spinnaker goes up and fills and then the pole is finally organized. Going onto a close three-sail planing reach, the pole must be set before the spinnaker fills; some crews set the pole even before hoisting the spinnaker. I think this is crazy, as it loses valuable seconds. When hoisting from a chute the crew should always help the hoist by pulling in three or four feet of spinnaker sheet. This eases the sail out of the chute quickly and also pulls the clews around, helping to avoid twisting. The crew should not pull too far, or the spinnaker will fill prematurely.

The guy should have either been cleated or be against a stop so that it is correctly set before the hoist. Once the spinnaker is set, the guy is hooked under the gunwale so that the crew can trapeze or sit out over it. This also helps to keep the pole off the forestay in strong winds by taking away a lot of the stretch in the rope. A limited amount of stretch is, however, desirable to let the pole go forward as a gust hits the boat and allows it to accelerate.

Once everything is set the helmsman must concentrate on the course and work every wave that offers itself. The crew's key functions are to keep the hull balanced laterally, keep the spinnaker drawing at its most efficient, and to use his weight and energy to ooch the boat through the waves.

Approaching the gybe, the crew will make sure all the sheets are clear and start furling the genoa if he considers it necessary. I have always preferred in all but very light winds to leave the genoa out as it prevents the spinnaker wrapping around the forestay, and helps to get the boat quicker on the new gybe while getting the spinnaker set.

In a good fresh breeze the pole should come across quickly, in preference to keeping the sail full. The helmsman should adjust the spinnaker sheet after the gybe, but must not fill the

With just a little pull on the spinnaker sheet everything would be perfect. Crew concentrating hard on his spinnaker while the skipper is able to watch the boats coming up on the beat and pick the best waves.

spinnaker if this prevents the crew getting the pole set.

Lowering the spinnaker can become one of the more anxious moments. Many well known crews have been seen sailing on past the leeward mark with the spinnaker stuck halfway down. The halyard must be free running, and before the drop the helmsman must make sure that he hasn't a snarl-up. Adjusting control lines for the next leg should be done before the spinnaker comes down. Good timing is the key; it is most important to round the mark correctly even if it means dropping the spinnaker early to make sure that all the sheets are out of the way, that the centreboard is correctly set and any adjustments to control lines are made. Rounding the mark inefficiently can lose in a few seconds all the ground gained downwind.

This sort of handling can only be achieved after much practice, and hours of preparation and thought in the preparation of the boat. For seven years I have had the pleasure of crewing many of the top British Flying Dutchmen helmsmen. I have been part owner of three FDs which I have been able to organize to my own way of thinking, and I have crewed others that, to my mind, left a lot to be desired. However, if you are really practiced with your own system, whether it is ideal or not, you are far better off than those who spend all their time going for the perfect system and never bother to spend the necessary hours practising around the buoys.

The most efficient forward spinnaker sheet lead that I know, I first saw on the Flying Dutchman of Geoff Smale from New Zealand. My version of this is shown opposite.

The next essential for speedy and efficient spinnaker setting is to have the pole height readily adjustable. It is no good having a system with a series of knots that necessitates the crew going forward to adjust the pole height. I violently disagree with Barry Dunning on this point, and feel that the knot system also necessitates the type of fittings on the pole that require the vang to be reattached to the pole after a gybe. His system may be all right for baby spinnakers, but not when there is a worthwhile area of nylon to control.

It is essential that gybing must be as simplified an operation as possible. If the guy is hooked under the gunwale it must release itself during the gybe. If it has to be unhooked, precious seconds can be lost. The vang must not be able to detach itself from the pole of its own accord; a simple hook and eye is probably the most efficient method. The hook should be incorporated in an adjustable system that gives one

The special spinnaker sheet fairlead and cleat developed from Geoff Smale's idea by Paul Davies. The sheet leads from aft through a lazy pulley and out between the two sheaves mounted above the cams of the jam cleat. Here the sheet leads aft as it would do in planing conditions with the crew aft. In light weather the sheet would run against the forward sheave. A knot tied in the sheet so that the spinnaker sets properly with the pole on the forestay allows the crew to cast it off on the gybe, when it becomes the guy and he has only the other sheet to trim.

Without a spinnaker chute this system obviously cannot be adopted as the sail has to be lowered into the cockpit. In that case the sheets must be marked for the appropriate sheeting position with tape.

Note the spare shackles carried on the retaining strings of the spinnaker launching chute.

lead back to the helmsman. Pulling this lead raises the pole, releasing lowers it. The pole only needs to be lowered in light to moderate winds when the elastic is strong enough. The downhaul wire must go to its end when the pole is in its highest position; this prevents it inadvertently skying in strong winds. The diagram on page 106 shows an adjustable vang arrangement.

If you are losing places downwind or rounding marks, analyze your problem. Do not pack your boat up after a race and suffer the same frustrations next time. Once you have

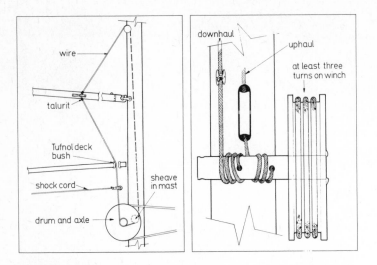

The efficient 'Paul Davies developed' spinnaker pole vang system. When not in use the shock cord with the small sheave at the end removes the surplus under the deck. The control of the pole is by the endless rope around the winch drum which has sufficient friction to keep the pole from moving.

The two wires are wound onto the axle in opposition so that one is tensioned as the other released.

Note: It is necessary to have two eyes in the wire just above the pole 'Talurits' with a small shackle in order that the mast can be taken out of the boat.
Courtesy Yachts and Yachting

perfected your system, practise until you think you are perfect, then look for something else to improve.

Postscript
Two top class crews, with different ideas on how to deal with some of the basic problems of spinnaker handling. Both have solved the problems. It is this freedom of thought which marks the really good crews. A fresh approach to a problem will often provide a much more efficient solution. Do not just copy the next man's gear—see if it can be improved on.

14
Spinnakers in Keelboats

The most significant difference between spinnakers in keelboats and those in dinghies is the size. Those on keelboats are bigger and thus need stronger gear and a lot more effort to handle them. Poles are bigger and heavier, sheets a lot thicker, winches appear and techniques alter. What one man could manage now becomes the province of two.

Because the pole is bigger and heavier it has to be controlled by stronger gear. Barry Dunning's bit of string with knots is no use on board a Soling, for instance, as he well knows. Once again it was Paul Elvstrom who developed the best gear on the market for boats of this size. The pole attaches to an eye mounted on a stainless steel collar lined with PTFE (Teflon). This collar can slide up and down the mast and is stopped by a nylon buffer at the maximum height. The topping lift and pole uphaul consist of a wire bridle attached to the centre of the boom and also to the collar. The attached line runs through a sheave by the spreaders and down the mast on a rope tail to a cam jam cleat so that when the pole is hoisted into position the topping lift is there also. The downhaul clips on the pole when needed and is also controlled through a cam jam cleat. The downhaul is removed by an elastic underdeck system when not in use.

What was quite common in the Dragon class was a rigid topping lift which needed no downhaul. It never found much favour because to adjust it the crew had to stand on the main boom to reach the mast end of the topping lift. However, I am working on a similar system for dinghies in the near future, but reversing the whole issue and having the rigid strut

underneath the boom. This attaches to a collar which slides up
and down the mast to adjust the height of the outboard end of
the pole. It works with a fixed eye on the mast for the boom
and an adjustable one for the stay pole on the collar which is
controlled by a double-acting winch system under the deck.
With this it will be possible to make hoisting, gybing and
lowering faster. The whole idea is readily adaptable to
keelboats, and if any manufacturer cleans up the gear
sufficiently he will be certain to clean up the market. This
system has the added advantage of keeping the forward side of
the mast clear and reducing the windage at a critical point in
the rig.

Halyards are invariably of flexible wire as they need to be
able to take the strain without the enormous windage of a
suitable Terylene rope. Since the wear on them is high,
particularly where they run over and emerge from the upper
mast sheave, they must be inspected daily. At the first sign of
stranding the wire must be replaced.

Sheets need to be larger to allow the crew to hold them to
control the larger area of the spinnaker, particularly in a stiff
breeze. However, there is no reason why they should not be
tapered. The value increases, the bigger the sheets involved.
Five thirty second inch diameter Terylene rope has a breaking
strain of a quarter of a ton which is perfectly adequate for most
day racing keelboats, and this spliced into three-eighth inch
diameter line where the crew holds the sheet and cleats it
would be ideal for a Soling or a Dragon. A light one-eighth
inch diameter plaited polypropylene sheet is a must for light
weather. Its effectiveness was proved to me when I sailed on
Golliwogs, Brian Saffery-Cooper's first Half Tonner. Whenever it got light this sheet used to be pressed into service and it
allowed the spinnaker to set without the weight of the sheet
dragging the leech downwards.

Snubbing winches were once considered necessary to
control the sheet in a breeze, but now the most common aid is
a ratchet block. They should be of the type which allows the
ratchet to be held clear of the block to run free for light airs. I
must admit there have been times in a Soling with the big
spinnaker up when I thought I was going to be dragged
through the block as a gust hit the boat, but after a time I
found ways of holding myself over the gunwale and fighting
the force of the spinnaker. At times in really heavy weather it
is quite likely that the crew may need two pairs of hands on the
sheet when using a ratchet block, but for all that, it is better
than having to use a winch on the sheet.

Because of their size spinnakers in keelboats are always

Helmsman, spinnaker sheet and mainsheet hands in full concentration while the 'bully boys' take a rest and use their weight most effectively in this Quarter Tonner.

hoisted to leeward. Unless they are up before they fill, the crew will have a struggle on their hands, and an uncontrolled spinnaker can soon take the mast out of the boat. If it should fill and the halyard is not in a cleat, for instance, it will blow out of the boat and take the halyard with it until the stopper knot hits the bottom sheave. Then it can easily go into the water and act as a trawl while the working sails keep pulling the boat forwards: in no time the mast breaks.

Spinnakers are generally hoisted from a plastic basket on the lee side. The pole is hoisted first, and with one person on the halyard and another on the sheets, the whole operation is relatively simple. As soon as the halyard man has hoisted the spinnaker he gets ready to help the spinnaker sheet hand where necessary. Heaving in on the guy when reaching in almost any breeze is a two-man job.

A keelboat can use a modified form of gunwale hook. A rope taken through a fairlead in the gunwale where the hook would be is taken to a jam cleat. A small block is spliced on the outboard end. The sheet can then pass through this block and the crew can haul the block, and with it the sheet, down as he wishes. This little gadget is also useful for keeping the sheets low when gybing to prevent them being hooked over the main boom end. To further prevent this, a length of nylon monofilament from the bottom batten to the outboard end of the boom, lightly tensioned with elastic, is most useful.

The spinnaker should always be doused to leeward as well. It can be collapsed in the lee of the mainsail by letting go of the guy, but on a reach the crew must be careful that the spinnaker does not remain full and act as an air brake. One man will have got hold of the sheet near the clew of the spinnaker, and as soon as the guy is released he will start to pull the sail in foot first; when the halyard is released he will bundle the whole thing inboard. The spinnaker sheet hand meanwhile has got the boat largely sorted out and will bundle the spinnaker into its basket as the forward hand gets the pole down and away. Its an all-action time and one which at first seems loaded with problems, but these disappear with practice.

All the principles of handling the spinnaker on a dinghy apply to keelboats, and there is little doubt that the weight of the crew as far to windward as possible does make the boat faster on a reach.

15
The Finish

The finishing line should be treated like any of the marks of the course. Just as many places are won and lost in the last few seconds as at any of the turning marks, and the crew and helmsman must be prepared to deal with situations as they arise. The finishing line will probably be shorter than the start line, but many of the principles applied to the start remain.

The crew's job is to make sure that the helmsman—who at this time is getting pretty tense—gets to the finish in the shortest possible time. He has to see which end of the line is nearest and try to make the skipper sail for that one. This, of course, can alter as they approach the line, due to a windshift. Because I was able to spot a shift in the fourth race of the 1972 Hornet World Championship, Simon Darney and I went from fourth to second with only twenty-five yards of the race to go. Three boats were within two boat lengths heading for the line, and because the pressures on the helmsmen were heavy not one of them noticed the slow change in wind direction that was heading them on starboard tack. As we were behind, the longer I could let them go on the better, and when I saw we could just lay the finishing line on port tack I called to Simon to throw around. He did so without question and we sneaked across less than three feet ahead of the other two. Since the winner of this race was subsequently disqualified on protest for an infringement at the start, this last minute burst gave us the race and put us in such a position that a win in the last race could win us the Championship. Had we finished fourth we would have been out of the running.

The rules state that a boat finishes as soon as any part of it or its gear crosses the line, but it is still under the rules until the last part has crossed. However, once the stem has been over the line there is no need to cross the line completely as long as it keeps out of the other competitor's way. It is important that crews should know these facts, because helmsmen are under heavy pressure at the finish and can easily forget. The boat must be driven as hard as possible until the finish line is crossed. I've seen many a place lost because someone gives up when they thought they had crossed the line and in fact had not.

I find that after the finish I want to pause, not from the physical effort so much as the mental strain. But this is the time to be careful: the majority of needless capsizes and subsequent mast breakings occur after the finish when people are not concentrating. It is so easy to relax and forget the simple things. The de-briefing can start, but the detailed examination is best left until later. Crews must make a note with the Chinagraph on the tactical boards of any gear repairs that have to be done, so that they aren't forgotten.

Skippers should encourage their crews to sail the boat back; that should keep them both concentrating until they get ashore.

16
From Dinghies to Twelve Metres
by Bob Bavier

More often than not I've skippered my own boat, and despite doing lots of crewing through the years, I've never considered myself a top flight crew. But one thing I know is the vital importance of skipper and crew working well together, and maybe a skipper's view of what makes a fine crew will prove enlightening.

There are certain qualities in crewing which apply primarily to dinghy racing, others to keelboats for day racing, and still others especially to ocean racing. While we shall consider each type separately, there are many common denominators and the qualities which make a good crew for one type of racing apply in large measure throughout.

Dinghy Crewing
It's not very exciting to start out by emphasizing the importance of good conditioning before you can be a good dinghy crew. By dinghy we mean not only the small one and two man open boats which earn the term in America, but all small racing boats up to about twenty feet. Here hiking is so important because these boats must be sailed on their feet in a breeze. Unless you're in great shape you just can't keep it up throughout a weather leg. People used to laugh when they heard Paul Elvstrom rigged hiking straps to his bathtub and spent long periods each day hiking out of it. They stopped laughing when Paul could sail a whole leg hiking continuously. Sure he was skipper as well as crew in his Finn, but the ability to hike is absolutely essential, and there's no other way to get ready for it than hard conditioning exercises. And

don't forget to condition your hands. Blisters don't make it easy to hold onto or trim a sheet. In other sports such as swimming and track events the amount of hours spent each day getting into shape has multiplied in recent years. The same is happening in sailing, and whether you like it or not it's becoming imperative to train hard in order to compete in fast company.

Condition applies to larger boats almost as much. While hiking is vital in a centreboarder, it also makes a Dragon sail measurably faster. And try grinding the coffee grinders on a Twelve Metre in a tacking duel or during starting manoeuvres if you don't think it's so important to be in good shape on a big boat. Obviously, it counts on ocean racers too where you've got to keep going for days on end.

Size is important in dinghies. Some small boats such as Tempests and Dutchmen need a big guy on the trapeze. It helps if he's tall, to give more leverage. Other small dinghies such as 420s, Penguins and the like bog down if the crew is heavy. There is not too much you can do about your size and weight, but if you want to be a good crew try to get a job on a boat your size is suited to.

Agility and coordination are also especially important in dinghies. That's something you're born with, but training can help. Whether agile or not, move slowly in light air in order not to rock the boat. Always be conscious of where your weight is. When tacking, it is particularly important to switch smoothly and precisely to the other side. Roll tacking in light air requires precise timing and should be practised. Speaking of practice, the race itself is a costly time to learn in. Effective, yes, but how much better it is to spend hours training each manoeuvre, spinnaker setting, and the like before a race. You will then gain valuable seconds in the race itself, and races are won by accumulating a few seconds here and a few more there. There's no mystery as to why America's Cup crews execute each manoeuvre, each sail change in such flawless, fast fashion. They have practised literally for months on end until the difficult becomes routine. The same practice will help a dinghy crew.

In small boats the crew becomes the skipper's second pair of eyes, sometimes the most important set. He should check the course signals and call the gun. Some skippers prefer to keep their own time, but more prefer to have the crew do it. It's vital that the crew know how much information, how much advice, the skipper wants. It's hard to overdo the information, but while some skippers prefer little advice, others welcome it. Tune yourself into your own skipper's thinking. Keep a sharp lookout for other boats, especially during pre-start mano-euvres. Look for wind shifts, new wind and headers, and report them. If you feel strongly on where you feel the boat should go, which tack to take, whether or not to sail high or low on a reach, etc., most (but not all) skippers prefer to have you speak out. It depends on large measure on whether the crew is a sound tactician and a skipper type in his own right. If he is, advice is usually welcome. But once you've given it, once you're sure the skipper has heard you and considered your advice, then shut up. There can be only one boss on a boat. Speak up again for your point of view if *new* evidence supports it.

Aside from calling wind shifts and puffs, it's also extremely helpful for a crew to keep the skipper advised on how he's doing relative to nearby boats. This enables him to con-centrate on boat speed and tells him whether he's in the groove or needs to change. But be sure you're accurate in this reporting, and be sure to report when your boat is doing badly, not just when she's clobbering the opposition. I recall when sailing *Constellation* in the America's Cup trials against *American Eagle*. Rod Stephens was my tactician and kept me posted on progress. I soon noted, however, that we always seemed to be beating *Eagle*, yet when I looked around we appeared little if any better off than before. I asked Rod how come, and he said he didn't want to upset me by reporting when I was not in the groove. Once I realized that's when I most wanted information, his observations were most useful and a big factor in our eventual victory.

Rod's reporting was even used on one occasion to upset the opposition. We were engaged in a tacking duel in one crucial race, with *American Eagle* on top of us. Rod was calling distances on the stadiameter to tell me how we were closing the gap. And since we kept closing, we continued the tacking. Finally we were so close to *Eagle* that the stadiameter could no longer record distances. Still Rod kept using it, and in a loud voice made such remarks as 'another ten yards, Bob' or 'one more tack and you'll have her'. It dawned on me that this reporting was for the ears of Bill Cox on *Eagle* in hopes of putting more pressure on him. Sure enough, he hurried a few tacks and we broke through, and I'm sure Rod's reports helped make it possible. It's just one example of how a thinking crew can help in unexpected ways.

In Larger Boats
Crewing in larger boats requires similar attributes but with several notable differences. Here the crew's primary re-

sponsibility is to work as a team, to do his job well in cooperation with others. A particularly able crew has to watch that he does not try to do everything himself. His first responsibility is to do his job well and to rely on his crew mates to do theirs. If he tries to do both, his job will suffer and a smooth evolution is impossible. Lots of practice helps on this, but if the time isn't available for practice each crew member must first find out what he is to do on each evolution. In finding out, if he thinks he can do still more, that's the time to speak out, but once the division of responsibility is established, stick to it.

Exceptions to the above will occur. For example, the crew members delegated to haul down the spinnaker might get in trouble and need help. If it starts getting in the water, that's the time for the crew to leap to assistance, but once the emergency is past he must return to his own post. To be most effective each crew member should know not only what his job is for each evolution, but also what everyone else's is. It helps emphasize the need for teamwork. While doing his own job, he should keep his eyes on the overall evolution and thus be ready to assist when someone else needs help. But if things are well organized and everyone does his own job, the need for further assistance is rare.

When first stepping on board a larger boat, the crew should immediately familiarize himself with it. Check where all the halyards, lifts, vangs and other items are. Know the place where winch handles are stowed, the location of reefing gear, spare lines and tools. Ignorance of these can really slow things down in an emergency.

On a large boat, should anyone other than the tactician advise the skipper? I feel he should, but usually in an indirect way. Say you're lying on the deck going to windward and see either a new wind, a shift, or the weather mark in the distance. If you're not sure the skipper or tactician has seen them, don't hesitate to report them. Since you are probably younger, you are apt to have better eyesight and hence there's a good chance that no one in the cockpit has seen it. So speak up. Usually it's best to report to the tactician who in turn can report to the skipper, but in any event don't keep information to yourself which could prove useful. Crews who are also skippers are particularly helpful in this regard because they have a feel for what's important.

There are times not to speak out and one is when the skipper is committed to a certain course of action. Remember also that since he is skipper, he just might know what he's doing, despite the fact that you as a crew disagree with him. Let me give you an example. During pre-race manoeuvres on *Constellation* we were going downwind on port tack, closely tailed by our opponent. It was important to gybe onto starboard in order to be able to return to the line on time. Our adversary was gaining, and an immediate gybe was imperative or we would be blocked. I figured we just had time to complete our gybe and gain rights and hence called for a gybe. The other boat was shouting to us not to gybe, merely to intimidate us, but when I called for the gybe one of my own crew shouted 'No, it's too close.' There was a momentary pause till I repeated the order to gybe. We completed it just in time, and the other boat did not have to start to alter course until after the gybe was completed and did not protest. But being questioned at this crucial juncture by one of our own crew was almost disastrous because it delayed the operation. And just imagine if they had protested how helpful it would have been to their case if they could have stated that even our own crew had said we were gybing too close! In short, in a tight situation remember there can be only one boss and its better to trust your skipper's judgement.

Teamwork on this Swedish Quarter Tonner—up forward the spinnaker sheet hand where he can best see the sail. The skipper forward so that he can see the waves, then the mainsheet trimmer and right aft the genoa sheet is trimmed.

The Ocean Racing Crew

Most of the above will serve the ocean racing crew, but there are some new factors which apply in particular to this type of racing. It is particularly important to know the boat, since you will need to handle halyards, sheets and guys in the dark. Know where sails, tools, reefing gear and emergency equipment are stowed.

It's important to pace yourself. When you're off watch either sleep or at least rest, otherwise it will be impossible to go all out for the hours you are on. But if a sail is torn and needs resewing, someone has to volunteer for the job and it might as well be you.

Keep yourself dry by putting foul weather gear on before you get wet. And avoid excessive sunburn. Too much sun can make you sick and a sick crew is no help. The same applies to seasickness. If you are at all that way inclined, take preventative pills before it gets rough.

In tough weather, and *always* at night, wear a safety belt and clip on while you're changing sails. The old rule of one hand for yourself, one for the ship is particularly true at night. Falling overboard can not only spoil your boat's chances—it can drown you, so don't be foolhardy. This doesn't mean that you should hesitate to go onto a heaving foredeck in a whole gale at midnight. If sail must be shortened or should be shortened, that's what you came for and it's all perfectly safe if you use your head.

A good ocean racing crew relieves the watch on time. He doesn't always head for the best bunk when off watch. He keeps trying every second, thinking of his four hours' watch as a race unto itself. He doesn't distract the helmsman but if he's good with jokes it helps to tell them at appropriate times. The old adage that a taut ship is a happy ship works in reverse. If the crew is happy, it's apt to be more efficient. I used to be violently opposed to drinking on any race. I now feel that *one* drink *once* a day is good medicine.

In closing, at the risk of sounding corny, there's one ingredient that all top racing crews have, regardless of the type of racing—that's desire. A will to win, a delight in hard work and discomfort in order to achieve victory, are attributes which any top crew must have. Fine to have fun, but never at the expense of the main purpose which must be to do all you can in order to get your boat home a winner. And for the dedicated crew an all-out effort is the most fun of all.

17
Some Thoughts on Keelboat Technique
by Adrian Jardine

I started crewing keelboats fresh from years of dinghy racing as both helmsman and crew. I began by applying my dinghy experience but found that while the ideas were in line with the boat's reactions, I had to modify my techniques simply because the boat and gear were bigger and heavier and took longer to react to trimming. I find that the knowledge gained in any form of racing can be applied elsewhere, but never in a dogmatic way. There is never a simple path to success, and neither is it true that what is successful in one class will be equally successful in another. I soon found that I had to adapt my ways to suit keelboats, and there is no doubt that adaptability is the keynote for all crews.

The first big difference is that quick movements of the crew weight makes less difference in a keelboat. Whereas in a dinghy weight is all-important, the effect of a lead keel so much overrides crew movements that for a time crews may wonder if their positions make any difference at all. This is more true when sailing in a 5.5 Metre, which is fairly heavily ballasted, while less so in a Soling where the effect of crew weight is proportionally increased. This does not mean to say that you should not sit a Soling out as hard as you possibly can— quite the reverse. The less effect overall that your weight outboard has on the boat, the more effect doing it properly will have relative to other boats.

Sail trimming, be it with the sheets or outhaul and Cunningham control lines, is slower in a keelboat because of the loads involved. The work load can be lightened by using more powerful tackles or winches, but then it takes longer because there is more rope to pull. Rapid movements of the helm tend to slow down a keelboat, so anticipation and appreciation of the wind and sea factors become of prime importance to the crew. The keelboat crew, therefore, has to be more aware of the effects of sail adjustments than his counterpart in a dinghy. In a keelboat the skipper is left to get the best out of the boat by driving it, concentrating on the wind and waves. His crew ensure that he gets the optimum from the rig.

Over the last few years leech tension has become the in phrase, but getting it right is what most crews have been struggling to do for years. There are many things which can affect the leech tension of the jib: mast rake, luff tension, position of the fairlead both fore and aft and laterally, and mast bend are all contributory factors and the crew must appreciate instantly which one, if any, is wrong for the existing conditions. He will have to choose between jib halyard and jib Cunningham, Barber hauler, sheet, fairlead control, backstay and even runners to get the best jib trim. He has to deal with the mainsail as well: Cunningham, outhaul, traveller, sheets and backstay are the major controls. So for any dinghy crew there is a lot of learning to do before he can reach a state of any competence in a keelboat, but he should have begun to appreciate the basic reasoning anyway.

Soon after his Olympic campaign in the Soling class, John Oakeley, the British representative in Kiel, said 'You learn more from crewing on a keelboat than you do from sailing a dinghy.' He went on, 'You have more time to take things in when sailing a keelboat and you get wider experience. All the problems with keelboats are bigger than with dinghies. Crews are more important, there are usually more of them, and they can upset a helmsman more in a keelboat if he has not confidence in them.' All very true, except perhaps that there is more time for the crew to take things in. Every second of my time is occupied because I think it is the crew's job to deal with the tactics in a keelboat. This needs the mutual respect and total confidence that John Oakeley talks about. Many of the top keelboat crews in international competition have been dinghy skippers and have more than a smattering of boat-for-boat tactical experience.

Teamwork on a keelboat has a more intricate set up than that on a dinghy and is equally important. In a three-man boat each man's duties are somewhat interchangeable, but routine jobs must be done in the proper sequence or the crew can get completely muddled. It is usually the forward hand who has the jib trimming to do, and the middle man who deals with the

The full effect of an inside overlap and good crewing can be seen in this incident. K95 has just overlapped 58 and the two crewmen on 95 work together to complete the gybe and get the pole across as the boat turns, so that once round they are both back in the cockpit to trim the sheet and guy and sail off with the windward advantage.

main and plans the tactics so that he can keep the skipper informed of all that is going on, particularly the movements of boats to leeward.

The forward hand is a particular breed of person. To be good he must be strong, surefooted and a complete seaman. He is responsible not only for the jib trimming, but for the spinnaker gear and packing the kite. He must also keep the skipper informed on what jib and mast settings he is using. On larger yachts the foredeck leader is the pivot around which the boat sails. He is responsible for the working of everything forward of the mast and for communicating with the helmsman.

Experience of working together is probably the most important factor for the success of any keelboat crew. Once a good working crew is assembled it is most desirable to stay together. Many things effect the good relationships of the crew; it is imperative that they get on well together ashore as well as afloat, and that their wives and girl friends do too. Paul Anderson and I have crewed for Robin Aisher in major international competitions for years but go our own ways in between to sail our own boats. We find that before we attack any new sailing project, we benefit from a 'think-in' ashore. Not one, but perhaps several before we even go afloat and then several more afterwards, so that we can plan the various routines and discuss the sailing problems of the boat. A crew that has been together for years will have confidence in each other and it does not take them long to get confidence in a new boat because they will all go over everything and check that it is OK. This is most important in really windy weather. It allows them to concentrate on getting the boat going fast and deal with the tactics, having no hidden fear of a failure of man or gear.

Keelboat tuning involves the crew as they have to help set up the rig. The first thing they will have to check is that all the adjustment tackles work properly and lead to convenient positions. Then they will check that the mast is upright, by seeing that the main halyard measures the same distance from each chainplate on both sides of the masthead. The sails are set and the boat sailed to windward. The jib is trimmed with a moderate angle of attack and leech tension to give an even flow that roughly corresponds to the side of the mainsail. Then the main is set up so that the leech forms a reasonably straight line and a check is made on the gap between the main and the jib to see that it is constant all the way up. When it is, the mainsheet traveller is trimmed until there is no weight on the helm. As a guide, aim for the neutral helm at ten degrees of heel or else the rudder will constantly act as a brake. Once this is organized concentration can be placed on fine tuning, experimenting with different jib angles and mast rakes. One golden rule is that only one alteration must be made at a time so that there are not too many variables in the later analysis of performance. It is often a combination of small factors that add up to the right answer.

The more upright a keelboat is sailed the better. This means sitting it out, but however this is done it is essential to keep out of the helmsman's line of sight. He needs an uninterrupted view of the wind and waves to come. In light weather the crew will probably have to sit to leeward to try to get a five degree heel to help the set of the sails and the boat's trim.

Racing with a spinnaker on a keelboat in a breeze is some of the most exciting sailing ever. The knowledge that if any member of the team gets his job wrong the boat will broach wildly keeps the crew on their toes. The spinnaker should be kept as far away from the other sails as possible, maintaining the luff on breaking point as it would be in a dinghy. The middle man should have the mainsheet and as soon as he feels the boat beginning to luff he should ease some sheet to keep the boat in balance. He and the forward hand work their sheets together while the skipper steers a median course between luffing in the lulls and bearing off in the gusts. On these legs the efficient crew will take yards out of the rest of the fleet.

I find crewing in a keelboat every bit as challenging as skippering a dinghy. There is more to do, but there is more time to do it in and get it right. You cannot accept a compromise, because the boat will be slower for it. Every demand of the boat has to be met by the crew who has winning in mind.

One of those times when the spinnaker is perhaps more harm than good. The stiffness of the jib helps it to hold a good aerodynamic shape, and by reaching back and forth a better speed can be made in little to no wind rather than trying to get the kite to set like this.

18
Catamarans

In a previous book written on catamarans in 1967 and putting a case for them in the Olympics, I wrote 'I think that 1976 will see a catamaran class in this blue riband of the sport.' Prophetic words indeed, but now the Tornado is in the big regatta, there will be an upsurge of interest in twin-hulled racing, and crews converting to cats from dinghies will find several major differences in attachments and will have to adapt their techniques.

Loads are very much greater in catamarans than in dinghies of equal length and sail area because the beam allows crews to apply tremendous leverage on the rig. Speed also increases the loads because the apparent wind speed is increased. Catamarans can sail to windward faster than the wind speed—taken to its extreme, the proa *Crossbow* sailed a leg of half a kilometre in the 1972 John Player World Sailing Speed Record Trials at thirteen point four knots in a wind speed recorded at only four knots. The sheer physical effort of sailing catamarans is greater than dinghies, and the crew will soon find this out in any breeze over about eight knots.

The pre-race preparation of a catamaran is similar to that of a dinghy except that the boat itself may have to be put together, as it is likely to be dismantled for trailing. However, the cat is unlikely to have a spinnaker and there won't be this complication to deal with. But there is nevertheless more work with a catamaran; there are two rudders and two centreboards to maintain, more hull area to keep smooth, and a trampoline deck to keep up to scratch. The latter will need the same sort of care as your sails and it has the disadvantage of both helmsman and crew jumping about on it all the time.

There's one job the crew will want to dissociate himself from, which is a regular catamaran chore. Sail battens are a most important factor in race-winning. Reg White's eyes light up as the subject gets around to battens. I should imagine that since he started racing catamarans he's spent more time making battens than he has with his wife and kids. Most people find it dull, hard work. No sooner is the batten planed near the desired thickness to obtain the correct bend than with one more shaving it has gone too far. That one has to go for scrap and another is started from scratch. Add to that the difficulty in getting the right wood, and it's easy to understand the fervent prayer that fibreglass technicians will get battens right for cats in the very near future.

The big disadvantage of a catamaran is its lack of manœuvrability. It takes longer to tack and needs a lot of help from the crew. However, the crew has a little more time on his hands when actually sailing and should handle the tactics in a catamaran entirely, while the helmsman gets on with the job of getting it to go as fast as possible. When tacking downwind, for instance, the skipper does not have to keep looking under the boom to see if he can lay the leeward mark: that should be the crew's job so that the skipper can concentrate on maintaining the rig just clear of the stall point.

At the start it's important to remember just how much ground a catamaran covers. A Tornado going to windward at twelve knots travels its own length every second. There is one advantage in that a twin-hulled boat can be started and stopped more easily, but it is essential not to be caught in irons—this can lead to being left badly behind. Should it happen, the jib must be hauled up to windward to get the bows to pay off, and then not let go too soon.

To tack well it is important to develop the timing. As the skipper puts the helm down the crew can come in off the trapeze and make his way to the leeward side quite rapidly. The jib should not be let go until it starts to back. Then it is sheeted in quickly and the crew gets out on the wire. In any breeze, unless it comes in quickly, even with a two-part sheet and a ratchet block the crew will have trouble getting it fully home. The lighter the weather the less quickly the jib has to be sheeted on the new tack. Cats, like dinghies, need that little flow in the jib to help them get moving.

On the beat the crew has to watch for other boats and windshifts. He must tell the helmsman if boats to leeward are pointing higher or lower so that he can plan where he wants to go. Tacking to cover another boat has to be considered very carefully because of the speed they will be going while you are stopped in your tack. Quite often it's only done to get them to tack back into an unfavourable windshift. Because of this the helmsman must be told of other boats before he makes his tack when the wind heads. The crew should learn how to judge when the windward mark can be laid as it saves the skipper the distracting constant over-the-shoulder look.

Going to windward in waves, it helps to stop the hobby-horse tendency for the crew to bend his knees alternatively so that his weight is moved fore and aft in opposition to the boat's pitchings. As the bow comes up the forward knee is bent to put the trapeze man's weight forward; as the bow drops he straightens his forward leg and bends the after one. The pitching must be dampened, otherwise the pendulum effect of the mast will take charge and will throw most of the wind out of the rig, and the boat will hit a wave with no real way on and stop.

In light weather the crew may be relegated to lying face down on the forward part of the lee hull deck. This helps to 'unstick' the weather hull and lift the two sterns clear of the water and reduce wetted surface. From this position he should be able to keep his eyes on the movements of the fleet and see any wind changes to leeward.

After rounding the weather mark there is a lot to be done, but it must be done in the order in which it has the greatest effect on the speed of your boat. The jib is eased first, then the mainsheet draft controls are altered, both downhaul and outhaul, to the set positions for the next leg. Finally the weather centreboard must be fully raised and the leeward one brought half up for a close reach. The broader the reach the higher the leeward board comes.

In strong winds on a close reach the crew will have to move right aft on the trapeze to prevent the lee bow burying. It is therefore essential to have a foot strap on the gunwale right by the transom for the crew's after leg. All the forces are trying to pull the person on the trapeze forward, and unless he is firmly hooked in he is bound to be displaced when the bow buries and the boat decellerates.

As the reach becomes broader and approaches a run, it becomes clear that unlike a dinghy a catamaran does not point anywhere near the direction it is finally aiming for. In any breeze over a couple of knots it pays to sail a cat downwind in a series of reaches, gybing to get the best windshifts. Both helmsman and crew must constantly watch the compass. As the crew's skill improves he calls off the course that they are making to the skipper, who can concentrate on steering. At each gybe the crew will have to drop one centreboard (the old windward one) and raise the other in addition to getting the main and jib across.

On the downwind leg the skipper will be sailing with the rig near the stallpoint, judged by the air flow across the mainsail, particularly on the lee side. It is therefore more important than ever that the crew does not over-sheet the jib. The tell-tales will give every indication of the flow, and all the sheets that can be freed should be let out.

Once the basic differences between a dinghy and a catamaran have been mastered, it is easy to develop crewing style in a twin-hulled boat, but it does take time to acclimatize.

K92's spinnaker went up with a twist and her crew will lose valuable time sorting it out. K96 already going well will get past before K92 can get her spinnaker drawing properly. A little more care with packing the spinnaker would have obviated this situation.

19
Sail Handling for the Crew
by Graham M Hall

The competent crew works to obtain an overall knowledge of sails and an understanding of their proper trim and handling. Sails are the engine, the horsepower, the drive for your boat—learning about your sails means learning how to get the most from your engine. All other aspects of boat speed are efforts to reduce unwanted negative conditions (drag, windage, weight, moment of inertia, etc.). Maximizing drive, therefore, is one of the prime crew functions.

The racing crew's most valuable role is not to act as an extension of the skipper's hands, operated on command like a robot, but to function independently to promote boat speed, trimming sails properly, instantly and correctly as the wind and sea changes, without the need to be directed. Downwind, the crew is primarily responsible for speed as he controls the spinnaker. Upwind, he controls at least half the ingredients of optimum speed, as he handles the jib and its related slot with the main.

So although the skipper has ultimate responsibility for speed (as he does for every aspect of the race), the competent crew can contribute significantly in the sail trimming department. The most successful skippers rely heavily on their crews to perform with perfection in their duties of evolution (tacks, gybes) and the fine tuning underway of the running and standing rigging for the maximization of boatspeed.

To learn some of the fundamentals of sail trim and handling, the aspiring crew can think of race day in four parts: rigging up, tuning, competition and de-rigging. We'll discuss some of the fundamental and advanced points in these parts.

Rigging Up

On the way down to rig the boat you are going to be asked to do a good portion of the work; carrying gear, bending sails, cleaning off the bottom. Don't worry if the skipper seems to be off talking with his competitors, or hob-nobbing around the bar. Your job is to rig up.

Remember that the sails are expensive and fragile. From the day they were bought the time is ticking away on their useful life. Every day of racing, every folding, every mistreatment shortens their productive span. Don't crush the sails, don't sit on the bags, don't drag them over rough pavement, don't get them wet if you can help it. Insert the battens gently so as not to stress batten pocket stitching—and always insert the bendy end of the batten first. When pulling a sail from a bag be sure the cord drawstring is fully open and knot-free. Forcing a sail through the narrow neck of a sail bag can cause permanent creases.

On a keelboat, stand with the jib between your legs on the foredeck and attach the tack first, followed by the hanks from foot to head, finally attaching the halyard and sheets. The main should be bent onto the boom first, then the battens put in, halyard attached and luff readied to be hoisted. The sail bags should be stored in a dry place: no sense putting a dry sail into a soaking wet bag. Always ask the skipper before hoisting a sail, and once everything is ready to go always look at the sail while it is going up. The tendency for a novice crew is to look at his hands or the winch instead of watching the sail. I had an enthusiastic crew once who pulled the headboard right out of a sail, and another tore a mainsail from luff to leech across a spreader when he didn't see the halyard forward of the shrouds. Both were concentrating on the winch instead of the sail.

Don't be afraid to ask the skipper to check your work. He'll be impressed that you're concerned with doing the job right—this is the important thing, of course, not that you feel able to do it all by yourself. The word crew means a team of you and your skipper. You are working together for the good of the boat. One of the important functions of the crew in regards to sail handling is to spot defects. Whenever you attach a sail, or handle a halyard, keep in mind that at some point everything wears out. If you can spot a frayed strand, or a worn seam in a sail, and bring it to the skipper's attention, it could mean avoiding a costly breakdown.

Once the sails are hoisted, be sure the various controls (outhaul, downhaul, etc.) are secured. These will normally be set up during the next stage of operation once underway, but before setting off they should be fast. Have yourself dressed for the day before casting off; you don't want to interrupt the tuning process by pulling on foul weather gear that should have been donned ashore. Check your sheet winches (ninety-nine out of a hundred turn clockwise) and coil the halyards loosely and without half hitches around the coils. Should the halyards have to be cast off in a hurry, you don't want a mess of spaghetti jamming into the mast sheave.

Tuning
Once under way, but before the actual competition starts, the crew enters the most worthwhile stage in his training as regards sail trim and handling. Tuning the boat for speed in a relaxed, non-racing atmosphere when the crew can ask questions of the skipper and learn what the controls actually do to the sails is his most valuable time. Perhaps there will be some one to tune against, another friend from the club with the same type of boat.

Putting the vessel in racing trim prior to the race should be a ritual practised every day. Arriving late and hustling out to the line just in time to catch the starting gun is harmful to boat speed and should be avoided. In fact, pre-race tuning sessions should be expanded to full practice days with one or several other competitors. It is in these sessions that a crew can learn the most in the shortest time. I know of no successful skipper who does not have revealing tuning sessions.

The skipper will normally put the boat on the wind, closehauled, free of backwind and disturbed air, possibly with a competitor on the same tack nearby. First the jib is set up. The halyard should be quite tight; certainly the luff wire should be as tight or tighter than the headstay. Sometimes the headstay itself may go quite slack, the entire rig hanging on the luff wire. One thing to remember is that overdoing the halyard may bring the mast forward, throwing the balance out. The skipper is in charge of sail balance, as he handles the tiller and can feel excessive helm. If there is weather helm the mast can be raked forward to help correct this condition.

In any case the sail itself should not scallop off between the hanks or sag excessively to leeward. At the other end of the scale, a tight roll of excess draft should not be pulled against the luff: the sail is then hoisted too hard.

The sheet leads are next. Generally the skipper will have an idea where they should be set, and on some boats they are permanently fixed. If movable, trial and error can be used to get the sail to set correctly. When the boat is turning slowly into the wind, the sail should lift, or luff along the leading edge, evenly. This assures that it has an even angle of attack to the wind. This aspect, the angle of attack, is the most important single factor in a sail's optimum speed. It beats draft amount and draft position combined. If she luffs first up top, bring the lead forward; luffing in the lower part requires a tighter foot, hence moving the lead aft. The in-and-out position of the lead, defined as the lead angle, again requires trial and error.

Generally it can be said that you want the lead in as close as possible without beginning to choke off the slot flow behind the main. If that happens, both speed and pointing ability will drop sharply. In heavier air you will normally sheet to a position further outboard, the wider slot being required because of the much greater volume of air passing through the slot. The exact position of the lead will be determined by the skipper through long experience and as such is beyond the scope of this chapter. The crew should understand what lead angle is, and what small changes are supposed to accomplish.

Which brings us to the most important part of this tuning stage. The crew should constantly train himself to 'look' for the shape of speed in the sails—especially the jib. Start immediately to look at the shape—the amount of draft, the position of the maximum amount. The slope of the airfoil curve coming off the luff—the radius of curvature of the sail across the middle—and finally the leech exit angle. As the skipper tunes and fiddles with the halyard tension, sheet lead location, sheet tension, etc. the crew must memorize the finalized shape of speed. Once found, it is extremely important for the crew to be able to reproduce that shape later in the race, and on different tacks. The skipper must be freed of having to check the jib shape after each tack.

Things to avoid are tight or hooking leeches—directing the flow right into the belly of the main—or a leech that twists off to leeward and flaps in the breeze. Also avoid the tight draft roll near the luff, mentioned above. In general, novice crews tend to over-trim nine times out of ten. In fact, even with experienced crews I have found that a slight lack of speed can most often be remedied by easing sheets an inch or less.

Another 'looking' job you can perform is to sight up the mast. Place your eye directly beneath the gooseneck so you have clear aim up the track. You can tell how much the rig is bending and in which direction. This is just another looking experience you can start doing in order to begin to be able to recognize the shape of speed. There will come a day when you will see something you know is definitely wrong about the sails or the mast and you can bring it to the attention of your harried skipper, and it just might be the thing that will save the race and the series. Believe me, your skipper will praise his lucky stars he has you.

Mainsail shape is primarily in the hands of the skipper on most boats; however, you may have the Cunningham (downhaul) controls forward. You may be asked to adjust the traveller, and the vang [kicking strap] is usually crew work. Learn what each of these controls does to the main by tightening and slacking them repeatedly during the tuning-up period while watching the sail. The outhaul will tighten the foot area and reduce the draft. The vang will tighten up the leech exit angle and turn the leech to windward. The traveler will move the leech bodily athwartships. The Cunningham or downhaul will reduce the amount of draft and move its maximum position forward.

Perhaps the most important control you will have is the jib sheet. Be sure to have a good mental picture of what the sheet does to the leech of the jib. It will be pretty obvious what it does to the luff of the sail: if you slack it out, the luff will flag, the wind blowing down both sides. What happens to the leech with that last inch of trim is much more subtle. If you must hike to windward and you can't see what is happening to the upper leech of the jib where it is close to the body of the main, get the skipper to move the sheet while you are down to leeward looking up. You'll be amazed how much the leech moves relative to the sheet. On a tall narrow jib like those on 5.5 Metres and Fireballs the leech can close with the main on a ratio of 6:1 with sheet trim. One inch of trim equals six inches of leech rotation.

The direction of pull in a high-aspect sail is nearly downward. In a long-footed sail the leech will move fore and aft to a greater extent with slight sheet trim changes. Another good time to see this movement is with boat tied up to a dock or on the trailer ashore. From a distance you can see much more than from the cramped quarters of the cockpit.

Another control you may find in your department is the mast puller (or pusher). This device is the same as mast 'chocks' or 'blocks' at the partners to restrain mast bend down low. If you have one, operate it while sighting up the mast to see the change in bend. If you have chocks, rearrange them and discover how many chocks equal how much mast bend. Don't confine your thinking to fore and aft bend; your mast will also bend to leeward above the hounds and to windward in the lower third.

One other place to sight up is from the forestay at the jib tack to the mast at the hounds. On a keelboat this is a lot easier than in a dinghy, but if you can do it I recommend that you begin the practice. Excessive sag can be seen, and after some experience the proper amount of headstay tightness can be determined. I should mention here that keeping mental notes to be recorded later in a notebook will do the aspiring crewman tremendous good. Jotting down things as you learn them tends to make the understanding of them much more permanent.

Another thing we are seeing more and more on sails is the tell-tale or stall pennant. These wool or Dacron yarns are taped or sewn to the sail (both main and jib) a short distance aft of the luff, and are used to read wind flow across the aerofoil. Since they are in pairs, one to windward and one on the leeward side of the sail, a reading can be had instantly of the overall air flow picture. The general rule of thumb is to move the sail toward the stalled side flow. However, remember to favour the leeward side—if you can't get both sides flowing, and both tell-tales streaming aft, then concentrate on the leeward flow, even if the weather pennant stands up straight. This will often be the case on the windward side of the main.

Besides being placed in the luff area of the sails, tell-tales are now also being put near the leech to determine if the flow is continuing across the entire sail. Even a single stall pennant attached to the after edge of a sail will give a good indication of total flow.

One of the most important subjects of practice sessions for the crew is setting and flying the spinnaker. I make it a habit to fly the kite once before each race. Just for a moment, with a gybe or two thrown in to get everybody warmed up. If your skipper doesn't, why not make a suggestion to him? Or get him to schedule a spinnaker practice session—he will sure be quick to criticize if your spinnaker handling isn't just right. Some hints on spinnaker practice would include setting without the pole, take down to windward, pumping in heavy air to promote planing, setting to windward, gybing and then setting, setting and dousing from the cockpit.

There are as many ways to pack a spinnaker as there are crews, but the important thing is to get it into the turtle without twists. Following down the luffs and across the foot will clear things up. Setting once and retrieving assures that a spinnaker packed into a chute launcher ashore will be set up correctly. I recommend that the retriever line goes to the outside of the sail, helping it to avoid a costly dive under the bow as the halyard is released.

Flying the spinnaker is a very important crew function. You are almost totally in charge of boat speed on the downwind legs, and a good spinnaker man is worth his weight in Harken blocks. Concentration is the key. Don't look around at the other boats; don't watch the scenery; don't get hypnotized by the water and the sun; don't let the chute collapse. Of course in a two-man boat you have to help with finding the mark (pick it out before you round the windward pin), keeping your skipper from fouling other boats, and staying cool. 'Keep that bag on edge' I tell my crews. All those force vectors should point forward, and the further out you can ease the sheet, the more flow around the spinnaker you will get and the more drive will be derived. The windward edge should be just curling, or starting to fold in. Carry a small amount of constant curl if you can. On edge means that you are going fast. On edge means that you are concentrating. On edge means that if you look away for two seconds the chute will collapse—and believe me it always will.

Keep trying to raise the pole to get the entire sail up into stronger air. The weather tack (pole end) should be slightly higher than the leeward clew at all times. If they are at equal heights, then the pole can most probably be raised. Play the pole in the puffs, raising it in stronger air, dropping it in lulls. In drifters, the pole will have to be way down to help hold the luff out properly.

Again perform your isometric 'looking' exercises. Look at the spinnaker's draft, its position, the shape, the wrinkles, the lay of the cloths, the threadline bias, stretch, luff tightness relative to the cloth just inside the tabling, head shape and foot shape. Stall pennants on the leeches and in the middle will be helpful to see wind flow. Note how the pole height changes the draft—higher means flatter, lower equals fuller. For some reason this is just the opposite to what a lot of novice crews (and skippers) believe.

Don't forget to get a healthy dose of gybing and dousing practice, either. Again, the crew can make or break the downwind leg, and you want practice to improve yourself.

Competition

Most competition, or races, can be divided into four parts: the start, upwind, downwind and the finish. A super crew will note his distinctly different jobs in each of these legs, and will learn to function efficiently.

For the start, here are a few pointers: stay cool, keep your eyes open, especially for the starboard tack or leeward boat the skipper does not see. Stay out of the way of the helmsman's vision while keeping good time, announced frequently to the skipper. If you are not flustered (your captain may be) you won't over-trim the jib—something that comes with fear I guess. An excited crew always over-trims. Rarely are you going tightly closehauled until the gun sounds, so keep the boat moving by being sure the sheet and the sail are out far enough—but not luffing. Concentration is paramount.

On the tacks, say from reach to reach, trim gradually as the boat comes into the wind, and then ease slowly as she falls away onto the other reach. Keep the power on as best you can unless you are told to kill way. Then let the sheet fly: be ready to trim again on command, but remember not to over-trim, the most common fault. Watch your tell-tails on shrouds and sails closely to determine wind direction as the boat turns, always keeping the sail perfectly drawing and right on edge. Don't stumble or jerk around in the boat. Think ahead about where you are going to place your feet and always move like a cat, keeping the boat at top speed, without wasting momentum.

Once the gun goes, again remember not to over-trim. The jib has to be right, not just tight. As you come off the line give your skipper reports on how the sail looks to you (after some experience) and how you think you are going in relation to the other boats. If you are slow, try easing slightly—it works most of the time. Jog the skipper's mind (which may be close to being burned out if it hasn't got a pretty good start) by saying 'How's the jib', 'How's the main', 'How's our weight?' (place fore and aft), etc.

Upwind is a battle of three parts: boatspeed, evolution and route. Immediately after the start you both search for speed by fiddling with the settings slightly until you feel things are optimum. Then as a crew you can help decide the route to take up the weather leg. Maybe you can see some shifts or better wind or something that makes one side of the course favoured. And finally, everything else being equal, the boat which tacks the smoothest will get to the weather mark soonest. Concentrate on the evolutions, the tacks. Move smoothly, and hold the jib sheet until the sail backs—pop it around and shift catlike to the weather hiking position, trimming sail into just shy of closehauled as the boat lays away. Once speed is regained (three, four seconds) or on command from the skipper, trim in to the true closehauled boat speed position.

Two major responsibilities belong to the good crew, on the upwind leg: don't let the skipper overstand, and don't let him foul out on a port tack or leeward boat.

At the windward mark there are many changes that the crew must help with as the boat is turned from a windward attitude to a downwind sailing angle. The sails must be eased out and made fuller, the spinnaker set, the mast may have to be angled forward and straightened. Making the sail fuller involves easing the downhaul or Cunningham, slacking the outhaul, slacking the backstay, and maybe even the halyard. The jib leads often are moved outboard to a reaching position, while the vang may need to be tightened or slacked depending on the boat. The vang can be over-trimmed causing an overly tight leech—especially in light air. The purpose of the vang or kicking strap is to maximize drawing sail area, by keeping the main boom from rising. The leech is kept from falling off to leeward and causing the power in the main to be lost.

The crew weight may have to be shifted. More often than not it will be aft, both in dinghies, to keep the bow from diving and to promote planing, and in keelboats to increase waterline length and therefore hull speed.

In preparation for turning the leeward mark all the settings must be returned to their upwind positions, of course. It is important to remember how much you slacked off so that things are just right for the weather leg. Give yourself plenty of time to take care of these adjustments. If you don't know how long it will take you, and how far from the mark you must start in order to get all things done—you should. The big dude at the helm will blame you if you don't finish—and don't ever, ever forget to put the centreboard down. Of course, in a keelboat it may be a little difficult.

Finishing is an important part of the race even though it is the briefest. Try to help the skipper determine the close end of the line, and be very careful of starboard tack boats coming up. Your tacks and control of the jib is more important than ever in a close finish, and remember that the sea will be somewhat more bumpy with crossing wakes, boats hanging around the finish line, and the spectator fleet milling about. It may be necessary to ease the sheets a very slight amount to be able to drive through the increased chop. Similar conditions may also be present at the windward mark.

Derigging
Once you have finished comes the job of de-rigging the boat. Don't let the boat as much as touch the dock or scrape on the beach. Don't get the sails wet when lowering them. Don't hit the skipper on the head with the boom when you drop the main. Don't disappear until the boat is washed off and properly put to bed.

The sails must be dried if wet, and properly folded in loose layers so as not to promote creases. A sail stowed wet will promote Melamine resin filler deterioration. The heavier the resin content (the heavier the stiffness of the material), the more liable the sail is to deterioration from wetness. Separate the sheets from the sailcloth if they are soaked. It is better to fold the sails loosely on the boat instead of stuffing them into the bags to be taken ashore and folded later. In fact, never stuff a sail—the thought of that makes me cringe.

Every so often the crew may be asked to wash the sails. The main idea is to keep the salt from building up. Even if the sail doesn't get get wet, it will strain the salt from the moist air and spray and soon get hard and stiff. Such a condition can cause crazing or cracking of the surface and should be avoided. If you can, hoist the sail up and hose it down, allowing it to hang there until it is dry, but only somewhere where it will *not* flap. If you must wash it on the ground, pick a clean piece of grass and scrub it gently with a brush and some mild detergent. Then hoist it if possible and rinse it off. Never put it in a washing machine or drier. The Dacron or Terylene material is heat set, and reheating the sails means re-setting it. The results may be astounding. Once I had a mainsail that would not measure in on the leech length. I told my crew to take it to the laundramat and dry it just a little—not too much, be careful, watch it, I just want it shrunk a very tiny amount, not too much. *Please* be careful. He melted the headboard. Needless to say the sail measured in. In fact the class measurer could not believe how much it had shrunk. Neither could I.

So you see that a proper crew has great responsibility toward the goal of winning sailboat races. Much of the secret of being a good crew is practice and 'looking' combined with concentration. The best boats always have crews with these qualities. The best crews are content with being a crew, for the moment, and are not thinking about how much better than the skipper they could do it. They're exhibiting a professional attitude toward their job, concentrating on doing their best as a crew and not worrying about the future. Concentrate, practice, look. And if you don't over-trim you'll be on your way to becoming a great crew.

20
Coming Ashore

Once ashore, helmsman and crew must immediately get on with derigging the boat and packing it away. If it is left until after your shower it always seems to be more of a chore. The crew that takes the initiative will do most of the work, but will find himself fully appreciated. Before any work is done the crew must make absolutely certain that his helmsman has signed the declaration. Even after he has been despatched to do just this, ask him again when he gets back because he may have stopped to discuss the race with someone and completely forgotten the purpose of his trip.

If the sails are dry they should be kept that way, and folded gently and put into their bags. If they have got wet with salt water they must be rinsed off and laid out somewhere to dry. They should not be hoisted and allowed to flap. There's only one type of person who benefits from this all too familiar sight of sails flapping for hours in the dinghy park and that's the sailmaker. A quarter of an hour's flapping will do more harm to sails than six hours of hard racing. Flapping the cloth tends to break the individual fibres and shake the resin filler out until the cloth breaks down and stretches badly. (There is also the likelihood that the sail will catch on a spreader or some other projection and tear or start a seam.) Sails treated with care will last an awful lot longer.

Sails should be examined carefully each time they are folded. The things to look for are any tears or stitching beginning to go, particularly at the corners or where the sails rub on the shrouds. These should be repaired as soon as possible. Halyards must be checked at the splices and where they are bent around sheaves. The kicking strap should be checked too. Look particularly at that part of the wire that goes around the winch. The standing rigging and particularly the clevis pins must also receive minute scrutiny. Any bent pins or wire that looks suspicious must be scrapped and replaced. When everything is tidied up, the boat can be hosed down thoroughly. It is left propped up by the bow so that it can drain and dry out. Then the helmsman and crew can go and get their showers and into dry clothes.

After the shower is the time to attack the jobs that need to be done. Girl friends can be pressed into getting some cups of tea and bringing them to the boat—or a drop of the brown and foaming for those who prefer it—while the sailors get on with the work. There is bound to be a whipping undone on one of the control lines, or a sheave that does not run as well as it should. The oil can is an essential part of any boat's equipment.

The rudder fittings and their bolts are a constant source of failure, sometimes with spectacularly disastrous results. It will not happen if they are checked frequently. It pays to get underneath and check the centreboard slot rubber. If this is torn or rucked it can slow the boat down appreciably. Warning of its failure may have occurred if the centreboard was difficult to move during the race. All the hatches of the buoyancy compartments should be unscrewed to let the air circulate. Rot will occur unless this is done. Buoyancy bags need checking to see that they are properly fitted and that their securing straps are OK. Sheets and control lines should be checked for chafe, and, if there is any doubt each suspect rope must be renewed. It's quite pointless hanging on to useless bits of rope, but don't throw everything away. Long bits like halyard tails can be cannibalized for other jobs. The good crew must keep his bosun's bag topped up with all he needs for renewals and refurbishing.

After the work is done and the cover is on, the crew and skipper can sit down quietly somewhere and analyse the race. They should try to look at their faults objectively and then they will be halfway to curing them in future races. A log of what went on from which something can be learned is forever useful. No one ever remembers just how each race went, only a few pithy highlights, but if it is jotted down it's there for reference.

One thing is important at the end of a race: it's good manners to congratulate the winning crew. He deserves the odd pat on the back.

21
The Woman's Problems
by Judy Lawson

I have heard, now and again, a pleased helmsman/husband turn to a competitor, generally one he has just vanquished to the crabgrass, and say 'You know where to find the best crews, old man? At the altar!' Needless to say, this remark is offered only after an especially successful day, on which you've ground down the currently hottest boat in the fleet on the final two mile beat; or gybed inside the leader in a Force six while he spun out and fell in; or, finally, after fifteen years of trying, won the class championship. Small but gratifying experiences such as these sometimes move a man to speak well of the crew/wife.

On the other hand, it would be neither edifying nor seemly to recount the comments of the same helmsman/husband at the end of a different kind of day.

The husband and wife, boyfriend and girlfriend, male and female skipper-crew relationship in a high performance racing dinghy is subject, I suspect, to some of the severest psychological and emotional stresses of any similar relationship in sport. It is a partnership capable of astonishing extremes, with high levels of competitive achievement equally possible with murder-and-mayhem, rending apart get-me-to-the-divorce-court-Charlie battles of the sexes. I am tempted to state as a general axiom, offered from the vantage point of half a dozen years in this position, that the size of the boat on which a woman crews ought to be inversely proportional to the closeness of her relationship with its skipper. But then, we are talking about dinghies, never more than twenty feet long and always boats that require physical closeness and teamwork.

Let it suffice as a warning, before I go any further, to note that the experience of racing a high performance dinghy in top competition, of sailing it well, and of winning together is not one that will smooth the ways of matrimony or spark a romance. On the contrary, the two roles—that of wife, fiancée, or girl friend on the one hand, and hard-working, hard-driving, hard-calloused crew on the other—are best kept as widely separated as possible. For the sake of preserving sanity, leave your racing problems on the water, and your lovers' quarrels ashore. Somewhere, I'm sure, there is a demonstrably loving, winning couple. But I have yet to meet them.

Probably as many female crews have jumped ship for yet another psychological tearing point, something I would call 'mental set'; a certain crystal-clear perception shared by skipper and crew of the level and intensity of effort they will expend on racing. I remember once hearing about how a really fine potential crew/wife, a girl who is quick, strong, and mentally acute, lost her job as trapeze hand by birdwatching when she should have been puffwatching. Considering the circumstances, a beautiful clear day in early spring, a Great Blue Heron soaring close overhead with the sun on his wings, one might easily forgive her distraction (which ended, dramatically, with a capsize), but sailing to win a race permits no lollydagging. My friend, the birdwatcher, is now shorebound. Her husband, an intense chap with a yen for international level racing, has hooked up with an ex-Olympian.

To appear less than totally dedicated, to make less than a *complete* effort, quickly marks one as just another Sunday pierhead jumper, or worse, a 'girl crew' called upon only when all available males are signed up and gone. I don't mean that one must pursue sailing with grim devotion to the cause-above-all-else, but any woman who truly wants to be a first class winning crew must hew to the line of ambition set by her helmsman. Indeed, she must often do more. To be always first at work on the boat, stowing gear, reading the race instructions, bending on sails is not too much to ask, but clear and tangible evidence of your involvement, which must match his own.

An equally important area of understanding concerns the *level* of racing to which one aspires. If the odd weekend of club series fills your competitive needs to a T, then don't go looking for a berth on a boat sailed by a would-be world champion. You might be very good indeed, in the opening rounds. But his frustration is bound to mount if, as the travelling regattas

Marc Pajot in F4809 takes the difficult way in to the weather mark, on port tack. His crew must tell him the right moment to tack to avoid KC4896.

come and go (in which he must sail if he is to hone himself against the best competition), your excuses for staying home grow ever longer and more colourful. It is very desirable, but all too seldom done, to spell out one's competitive goals. Sacrifices of many kinds are involved in serious campaigning, and you ought to weigh them up before committing yourself to a boat and helmsman for a year or a season.

There is another side to this proposition. Occasionally a crew may find herself, inadvertently, riding around in the pointed end of a vessel being steered for no greater glory than a mid-fleet finish in the Nether Marshes Sailing Society Annual Reach-Around. Harden your heart against this helmsman's pleas to stay on for more. For more, in his case, can only be less, and less each year as his casual, fling-round-the-buoys-with-a-beer-in-each-hand approach drops him ever further back. If you feel mismatched, get out. There's neither fun nor gain in riding around with this Neanderthal of the Backwaters while you dream of gold medals and silver salvers. Having mutually agreed, mutually perceived goals is an important part of the wordless rapport skipper and crew should strive to develop. Twins seem to be most fortunate in this way, being all but clairvoyant at times, and have you ever counted the astonishing number of twins and brothers among the winners of class championships?

Having thus dealt with what seems to be the primary psychological hazards encountered by the female crew, I shall move on to the much less important practical and technical ones. Such as the smaller size, weight and strength of the female of the species. There are a few women who have none of these natural drawbacks. You may know one: she is near six feet, one hundred and sixty pounds or so, well-distributed and mainly on the upper parts of a slimmish figure, with the length of limb that equals sheet-tending more surely than bulging triceps. Whenever I view one of these blessed Amazons, which is usually at a cocktail party or on the beach, I wonder wildly why she's not trying out for the Olympics, or a well-known face at the top of some hot international class or another! I am purely envious, being an ordinary five feet seven inches and a hundred and forty pounds myself. Have a look over the crews of any major FD, 505, International 14, or Hornet meeting: with few exceptions, they are tall, long-limbed, wiry . . . and male. Through some pretty simple deductions I have come to believe unswervingly that but two things stand between any tall, strong, athletic (but female) crew and a fair crack at sailing on top boats. First, there is the sometimes real, but mostly imagined, male chauvinism that tends to scare women away from the tougher kinds of boats. Second, such a girl may be, despite her excellent physical equipment, not sufficiently motivated to compete at this level. C'est la vie, but what a shame, what a waste!

Most women, at any rate, are not rightly built or at least not ideally built for crewing a super high performance boat. But if that's your thing—if swinging from the wire of an FD (which, with its enormous genoa is the least practical), 505 or 14 turns you on like nothing else—you're probably going to do it anyway and not be put off my mere physical limitations. You *can*, however, grow stronger and, to a point, heavier. If I sound like a dyed-in-the-wool positive thinker, let me assure you I am. It's been drilled into me by that Man in the Back of the Boat (when the centreboard pin saddle jams and only Hercules himself could budge it, or we are about to change spinnakers for the fourth time—from the wire—on the same wild reach) he'll intone: 'If you *really* want to, you can do it.' It's said a person can lift ten times his (or her) weight, if the desire is strong enough.

Sheer muscular strength is an over-rated virtue in dinghy sailing, however. The physical condition for which the female crew should strive has two more important components, cardiovascular fitness and muscular endurance. Ratchet blocks, high-powered winches and sophisticated sheeting systems with smooth-turning ball-bearing blocks have taken much of the back breaking out of sailing. But if one is to sit or hang out with maximum effectiveness over say a fifteen mile course, staying power is essential.

Unfortunately, sailboat racing is one of those peculiar sports which while making occasional extreme physical demands, does little toward developing overall fitness. Unless you go out every day, in all winds and weathers, a la Paul Elvstrom, your muscles, lungs and circulatory system get minimal and sporadic working out. A conditioning programme outside of sailing is called for.

Look for other sports or activities—running, swimming, cycling, tennis, even walking—to get in shape for sailing. All the aforementioned will develop your body's overall efficiency, provided they are done vigorously and often. A programme I followed for about six months prior to the Internationally World Race Championship in 1969 consisted mainly of running about three miles every working day to and from my downtown office, and dashing up and down twelve flights of stairs at lunchtime. Total time expended was less than forty-five minutes. Eventually I even got to ignore the stares and occasional whistles of other pedestrians along those city blocks! Each of these activities is fun, or can be if you approach it as such, and only swimming (in a pool) and cycling (on a bike) require a major investment in equipment. The results of a regular, vigorous exercise programme are increased mental as well as physical toughness.

Calisthenics is *not* a dirty word. They will not distort your feminine curves into muscle-bulging protuberances. These exercises, designed to build muscular endurance, are perhaps the most important means by which the female crew can build the long-winded, stretch-driving strength that is one of the real keys to gold in a sport where championships are often won and lost by inches. The female back and shoulders seem always to be the weakest areas, and a programme of exercises aimed at strengthening these muscle groups will make you more desirable not only on the race course, but in social situations where appropriate dress runs to backless, halter-style gowns or skin-tight jerseys. You can probably name others, but the good old push-up, chin-up and weight-lifting (don't panic, I mean frequent repetitions with light weights) all work. For the lower back and stomach muscles used in sitting out, I've been told that the bent-leg sit-up is more effective than one with legs straight. Trapezing seems to be hardest on the legs, particularly thigh muscles, but these get worked out in the cardiovascular exercises such as biking and running.

Either way—trapezing or sitting out—a good female crew ought to be able, *and not afraid*, to carry additional weight when the breeze comes up. This also requires muscular endurance that must be worked up to, for the added ballast is supported and moved about by the same old body. From carrying originally around ten and then fifteen pounds of 'wet sweats' I've achieved the ability to carry, comfortably, about twenty-two or twenty-three pounds (in a much better designed vest) on the 14. While twenty-two pounds may not seem like much (the international rule sets the limit at fifty-five!) it makes a considerable difference in the feel on the helm of a light dinghy, and enables the helmsman to bring in the traveller and reduces the need for feathering. Don't discount the impact on your rivals when you casually doff this extra weight, heaving it to a friendly race officer between starts when the wind sighs off to a gentle Force three. Never, never set off for a race wearing a weight vest heavier than you're accustomed to. You must practise with the thing on first, for if it tires you too quickly, or inhibits your freedom of movement more than slightly, the whole advantage is lost.

General fitness also helps coordination, the speed and

efficiency with which you move around the boat. And this, at last, allows me to touch on the female crew's few natural advantages, one of which is agility. Another is sensitivity to the trim of boat and sails, the feel of windshifts, puffs and let-ups. A third, sometimes, is the othertimes *dis*advantage of relatively light weight. If one is quick and nimble, sensitive to slight changes, and light on her feet (and on the rail or wire) she probably has the all-round muscular coordination to crew a dinghy well. Exploit your strengths, madame. Take this well tuned, finely adjusted body of yours and turn it into an instrument for top boat handling. The roll tack, marginal plane (when your light-footed precisely balanced move aft gets your boats up and going while the heavy brigade wallows astern), light air gybe from forward of the mast, and perfectly timed all-standing planing gybe are your forte. You can, in a sloppy seaway, concentrate your weight more effectively by trapezing directly over and behind the helmsman, straddling him with your legs, to help reduce pitching. Try standing on his shoulders sometime!

A fit female crew *ought* to be able to outmanoeuvre most men in a typically small, confined racing dinghy. Assuming, of course, she is of average size and not our enviable six foot Amazon who will probably get hung up on the vang. She should work on developing timing, for like musicians very good dinghy sailors learn to orchestrate their moves to each other so that, for example, as the skipper moves in the crew extends further out, keeping the boat on a constant angle of heel. If gymnastics coaches may be believed, girls concentrate better than men in sport. Precision timing is, I think, the result of sensitivity combined with concentration and practice.

The location of adjustments for sails and rigging is sometimes said to be the most critical factor determining whether a woman can crew a particular boat successfully. To an extent I would agree, for those adjustments that demand the application of considerable strength or leverage should be placed for the helmsman to operate. For example, the centreboard lift and/or downhaul, perhaps the main Cunningham line. But with the little 'black boxes' developed recently, most of them with a mechanical advantage of six or eight to one, fingertip control of mast rams, jib halyards, outhauls and such as arrived. In any case, on any boat the crew must have authority to make changes in the location and functioning of all controls in the forward end. A female crew worth her salt will learn to use and accurately set every control on the boat, paying particular attention to those that work stiffly. There are no more dreadful, blood-chilling words of failure uttered by a helmsman than 'come and take the tiller', as you struggle for anguished moments with a stubborn piece of rope or metal, frozen in its tracks. And five boats race by, and The Cup is lost.

You are both, after all, there to win. I remember the Prince of Wales Cup in 1970, when Jeremy Pudney and crew Peter Brazier won in an eighty boat fleet, not on boat speed but through the most extraordinarily fine boat handling and tactics. 'They won', observed Stewart Morris, 'because their sailing was faultless.' *Their* sailing. A sterling accolade indeed from a man who has won twelve POW Cups.

Every class has, I'm sure, its own version of The Crews Union. The International 14s claim one of the oldest, if not most vociferous, Unions. Its emblem is the plain blue tie, modestly embellished with a fouled anchor in red and white. The white symbolizes sweat; the red blood. The Union's motto is not fixed, but seems to alternate between 'Confusion to our enemies' and 'More beer!' Despite its members' liking for a practical joke, it is an organization of high purpose and serious intent. As the 1969 14 team racing drew near, I recall expressing my reverence and awe for The Union to my helmsman. His reply 'You know, they don't take women.' I knew. Toward the end of that series I was initiated into The Union, which act must stand forever in my memory as a landmark in desegregation, and is probably the chief reason for my continuing loyalty to the Forward End of the Boat.

For in the end and ultimately most crews aspire to The Helm. Should one fight this craving? It depends. My own ambivalence is rooted in a very genuine liking for crewing, while at the same time I appreciate the pleasures of command. The crew race, wherein helmsman and crew trade places for one, usually the final, race of a series may be an American quirk: I'm not sure. It seems to be a healthy thing, especially for the helmsmen. For some crews it is the beginning of the end. Never having known The Power of Command, they have never known the need for it. For most, however, an occasional turn at the helm is a necessary part of the learning process, and surely the best way to appreciate the problems in the other end of the boat.

Just because she happens to be a doe among gorillas, a girl crew should never back down from a crew race. ('The two-part traveller's too much for you, dear.' 'What *will* you do if we capsize?') It is, in fact, more important, if anything for the female crew to seize this initiative. Her aggressiveness is more likely to command respect than jeers. I would never recommend taking the helm as a sort of 'women's lib' gesture, however. Although someone with a PhD in psychology is probably going to make an issue of this, I would stress that encouraging women to crew and skipper high performance dinghies has nothing, absolutely nothing, to do with the so-called feminist movement. The sport of racing small boats has been dominated by men purely by circumstance. There is nothing here to be liberated. As soon as there are one or two light, small, but high performance two-man (or woman) dinghies included in the Olympic classes line-up I think that girls will be there. Encouraging women into such classes has come, in fact, to be one of the arguments put forth by proponents of more dinghy classes in the Games.

To wrap it up: there are a few minor but useful thoughts concerning female dinghy crews I should like to pass on for whatever their small worth. It seems simplest to put them in the form of rules.

Don't wear jewelry out sailing. It catches on things.

Keep long hair plaited or under a cap. It also catches on things. (There was once a lovely girl, whose long curl caught on the wire. On the tack, her skipper (and sire) shouted 'Timber', chopped it off. All of it.)

Don't wear father's or brother's cast-off baggy shirts and sweaters. They catch on things.

Invest in some sleek, close-fitting sailing clothes, particularly a good wet suit.

Don't wear makeup unless you don't care about looking like Dracula's Daughter by the end of the first reach. You are a spray shield.

Get suited up before reporting to rig the boat. Saves time later, when your helmsman may be in a great rush to get afloat and certainly not happy to have you run off to the loo for last minute adjustments.

Have several long evening skirts in your wardrobe. They cover bruises, besides being warm and pretty.

At the end of the day, pack up the boat before you socialize.

Get fit.

Keep fit.

Know the rules.

Think ahead.

Forget that you're a girl.

You *can* do anything.

Vive la difference!!

It should never happen, but it does, and when it does there are always complications. In this case the plate has gone back up in the box, there is danger of the boat blowing onto the lee shore, and the spinnaker has somehow got twisted. That twist will have to come out before it is pulled down into its chute. And all this happened when they were leading.

22
The Capsize

It can happen in a flash, it can happen slowly; but one thing is certain—one day you will capsize if you race a dinghy. In the early days beginners will probably think they have joined a swimming club and not a sailing club, but as proficiency improves the frequency of immersions will reduce. The very best people capsize, so it is nothing to be ashamed of. I saw a whole lot of them at the British Olympic trials for the Flying Dutchman class and there was even one at the Olympics at Kiel—and that was strictly a light airs event.

There are many causes of capsizes, but most can be attributed to carelessness or a fall-off of in concentration. Helmsman or crew can be equally responsible.

When it happens there is no need for panic, but under no circumstances must anyone leave the boat. The safety of a small boat sailor is infinitely greater if he stays with the boat no matter what happens. The only case of drowning that I have been anywhere near occurred when someone decided to swim for the shore, rather than stay with the upturned boat. When capsized, helmsman and crew may think of all sorts of reasons why they should leave the boat at the time; but when these are analyzed afterwards not one of them is valid.

Rarely is a capsize unrightable. I have only ever had one that proved so, and that was at Shoreham in a full gale. The boat was blown off the top of a wave sideways into the trough and nothing the helmsman or I could do could stop it from being blown over. In the troughs the mast was touching the bottom and very soon was badly bent at the hounds. Consequently, as the two of us tried to right the boat we were working against a vast scoop made by the mast and mainsail. We tried to get the mainsail down, but it was jammed by the kink in the mast at the hounds. We even tried to get the mast down, but we couldn't get at the shroud plates with a screwdriver in the seaway, and the rescue boat hadn't any bolt-croppers to cut the shrouds. After well over an hour we were both exhausted and the boat was being carried towards the surf inshore. We had to abandon our dinghy for the rescue boat, and even our tow line parted. The boat then was dashed against a breakwater—there is one every four hundred yards or so along that shore—and badly smashed.

We did learn one or two things from that experience. We were on our own for over half an hour (the rescue boats had seen us but were busy with other boats), but were completely unworried because we stayed with our boat. If we could have got to the pliers (stowed under the foredeck) maybe the side cutters would have eventually gone through the shrouds and we could have got the mast down. The sacrifice of one shroud could have saved the boat, and the mast would only have needed a new top sleeved and welded on; as it was we lost the lot.

After most capsizes the main thought is to get the boat upright and back into the race. If the crew can get onto the centreboard quickly he will stop it from turning turtle. If he doesn't, the problems are greater. The boat that has gone in to windward provides righting problems. It may first be necessary to right it and get a subsequent blow over the other way. This can be quite spectacular for those watching, and exceedingly aggravating for those in the dinghy.

If there is any doubt, the crew's job is to go to the stem and swim the boat's head into the wind. Then the helmsman has a relatively easy task standing on the centreboard, jib sheet pulled up to its stopper knot in the fairlead, and he leans back until the boat comes upright. He gets in and sorts out the mess, and the crew gets in on the weather side when the skipper can head off a little. Unless both helmsman and crew are very light they do not both need to be on the centreboard to right the boat. It is quite possible for two people to break the board if they try.

One time when two may be needed is when the boat has gone right over. The technique then is to take one of the jib sheets and pull it out until the stopper knot is in the fairlead; then with both standing as close to the other gunwale as possible they lean back and pull on the jib sheet. The boat will come up slowly at first. When it is nearly on its side the helmsman will get his weight onto the centreboard and the crew will go to the stem and swim the boat's head into the wind, and from then on everything is relatively easy.

During a heavy weather race a lot of capsizes occur at the gybe mark. Often a whole string of boats go over like a deck of cards because each one has to take violent avoiding action and the crew is not prepared for the helmsman's movements. Under these conditions the crew must keep a sharp lookout and save himself from becoming one of the pack.

Capsizing is not the end of the race, or at least it should not be. A dinghy can be up and going again in under half a minute and lots of races are won by less than that. Even a couple of flips need not be disastrous. I have been in the winning boat that's had three capsizes and the second boat none at all. We were living dangerously while the other played safe.

A good lifejacket is essential, and it inspires self-confidence. Even if the crew finds himself under the sail, he has no need to worry. A sharp push upwards and he will get some air, and the nearest edge of the sail is less than six feet away, wherever he is underneath. There is no need for panic: capsizing is purely an embarrassment.

The Swedish crew is going to save this situation for his skipper. Having gained an inside overlap the US boat's crew has messed up his spinnaker by not cleating the old sheet before the gybe. Now it has become the guy it should be, the prime control of the sail as the one on S2533 is. The Swedish crew is in the process of clipping the pole to the guy and in five seconds this boat will be at full speed and sailing away from its American rival.

Everything in balance and the sails drawing well. Crew supported nicely by his trapeze to windward has perfect view of the sail he is trimming. The genoa is working and the boat is bolt upright—perfect.

23
The Final Analysis

A good crew is dedicated. He will have been involved with the boat's preparation long before it ever went into the water. He will probably have put in more hours than the skipper both on and off the water before the season is over. He is familiar with the rules, both those that concern the boat and the racing ones, and can probably out-talk the skipper on most. He will be as familiar with the boat's trailer as the boat, and is doubtless the custodian of the tool box. His sense of humour will have maintained the balance of compatibility in the boat and his long suffering will be shared among his fellow crews.

It's not a dismal picture, as he will enjoy his racing and will have fought hard to get his boat to the front of the fleet. He will have been praised, cursed, cajoled and bullied and done the same things in return. He will certainly have developed one or two faster systems to handle the sails or gear, and perhaps by the end of the season collected a few trinkets in the way of reward. He will, however, be appreciated for his talents; no longer does the lord/serf relationship persist.

The crew's education may well have reached the stage where he considers it beneath his dignity and rushes off to buy his own boat. All very well, and a great deal of useful experience he will glean for when he returns to crewing, as inevitably the good crew will. The one thing that the crew can do effectively is control the sailing of the racing boat. By the time he has found how this affects the boat and dismisses all those habits which are detrimental, his role is cast. His ideas are those which are a major contribution, and so is his ability to put them into practice both afloat and ashore when working on the boat. His ability to analyze mistakes and find ways of correcting them will count towards any boat's success.

Experience is the keynote, and the broader that experience can be the better. Several helmsmen keep the same crew through many different classes. Other crews stay put in the class they know and join up with a new skipper every couple of years or so. There are still others who change classes from time to time, picking their new skippers with as great care as Arnold Palmer would choose a new club. All benefit from change, but the change should not become the most important factor. Some campaigns take three years or more, and anyone embarking on the ultimate—an Olympic effort—must realize that three years as a team is just about long enough.

Pleasure for the crew will have been proportional to the effort he put into his racing. When a fitting fails during a race it will have been because of neglect in maintenance or an incorrect choice in the first place. The crew who does his homework will have few gear failures, but it will have meant a lot of hard work.

The good crew stays crewing because he likes it. He knows the tribulations, but he also knows the joys. He will often help the newcomer, but only so far—he doesn't have to give everything away, although the observant newcomer will soon be able to find out most of the tricks of the trade by watching the experienced old hands. Seamanship still wins races. It was an old adage of the paid hands that 'any fool can pull on a sheet but it needs a seaman to ease away.' It is still true. Bullheaded brute force is useless in a racing boat; appreciating what one is doing and what effect it has on the boat is the hallmark of the good crew. Racing is fun and there is more fun in winning; there is no substitute for success and there is no easy way to achieve it.

Appendices

A Checklists

Before going afloat
The bottom of the boat has been washed clean.
The centreboard gasket is intact and there are no foreign bodies in the centreboard case.
None of the rigging is fraying and all the shackles and clevis pins are done up and split pins are taped.
Weather forecast
Course
Tide times and direction of flow
Sign out if necessary and check noticeboard.
Check that the following things are in the boat:
Sails
Sheets
Battens
Spinnaker boom
Bungs
Anchor and warp
Paddle
Bailer and sponge
Trapeze harness
Protest flag
Instant repair kit: (2 fathoms $\frac{1}{2}''$ Terylene, shackle, knife)
Necessary tools—screwdriver, pliers etc.
Pair of Polaroid sunglasses.
Check your clothing:
Have you enough sweaters?
Lifejacket
Oilskins
Wet suit
Gloves
Check that you have a course card and a set of race instructions.
Check that the halyards are free and the sheets not fouled.

15 minutes to the start
Clear unnecessary gear from boat and put spare sails etc. on
committee boat.
Check compass bearings to first mark and of start line.
Check direction and state of tide.
Make sure boat is perfectly dry.
Stow everything properly.
Get skipper near committee boat for 10 minute gun.
Check centreboard for weed.
Get him to check for weed on the rudder.
Check sail trim and set correct for first leg.
If other classes starting ahead watch who does best from the
start and where they started.
Find the right end of the line.

10 minutes to start
Settle the helmsman.
Check sail trim and set correct for first leg.
Get accurate check on five minute gun.
Count down in minutes.

Last 5 minutes to start
Check centreboard for weed.
Get helmsman to check for weed on rudder.
Watch other boats around and inform skipper where
necessary.
Keep countdown going in half minutes to last two minutes,
then 15 second intervals until 30 seconds to go. Then give 25
and 20 seconds, and every second thereafter.
Watch line in case of 1 minute rule.
Make sure skipper is close enough to line.

Immediately after the start
Check that there is nothing to stop boat going at maximum
speed.
If skipper is pinching—tell him.
If he is falling down in another boat's dirty wind—tell him.

On coming ashore
That the skipper has signed the declaration or completed
whatever formalities are necessary.
The boat is washed down and the sails hosed.

After changing
The sails are dried.
The boat sponged out.
All the things that failed during the race are put right.
The cover is put on and the boat lashed down.

B Gear Recommendations for Dinghies

Wire rope

Shrouds	$\frac{1}{8}''$ diameter	1×19
Trapeze wire	$\frac{3}{32}''$ diameter	1×19
Halyards	$\frac{1}{8}''$ diameter	6×19
Kicking straps:		
standing parts	$\frac{3}{32}''$ diameter	1×19
running parts	$\frac{1}{8}''$ diameter	6×19
Sail controls	$\frac{5}{64}''$ diameter	7×7
Spinnaker boom vang	$\frac{5}{64}''$ diameter	7×7

Ropes

Mainsheet	$1\frac{1}{4}''$ circ. matt plait tapered to $\frac{1}{2}''$ circ. plait
Mainsheet traveller	$\frac{7}{8}''$ circ. matt plait
Jib sheet	$1\frac{1}{8}''$ circ. matt plait
Spinnaker sheets	$\frac{3}{4}''$ circ matt plait tapered to $\frac{3}{8}''$ circ. plait
Sail controls	$\frac{1}{2}''$ 3 strand or plait
Sail controls where force needed	$\frac{3}{4}''$ matt plait

C Flag Signals

Class flag 1 gun	10 minute signal
Class flag and Code P (Blue Peter) 1 gun	5 minute signal
Code 1 and Sound Signal	One minute rules (round the ends) in operation.
Flags dropped 1 gun	Start
Class flag held at dip 1 gun	Recall for one or more boats
1st substitute 2 guns	General recall
Answering pennant 2 guns	Postponement
Code N 3 guns	Cancellation or Abandonment
Codes N and X together 3 guns	Race abandoned but restart soon
Code O Regular Sound Signal	Change of course—race in progress
Code M	On a boat replacing a mark of the course
Code B	Protest flag
Code A	Boat has divers working around—keep well clear

D Contents of the Bosun's Bag

Contents of the crew's 'bosun's bag'
Some crews carry the whole tool kit, but I feel this is really the skipper's responsibility. The good crew should have a bag of specialist bosun's tools for the day-to-day running repairs and of course the ability to use them.

1. Sailmaker's palm
2. Sail needles, sizes 10, 12, 14, 16. Keep them in a small flat tin.
3. Reel No. 8 beeswaxed Terylene (Dacron) thread
4. Reel of fine Terylene whipping twine
5. Reel of sailmaker's Terylene sewing thread
6. Block of beeswax
7. Block of paraffin wax
8. Assorted shackles (stainless)
9. Clevis pins (stainless)—all sizes with retaining pins
10. Tin of assorted nuts and bolts with washers
11. Marlin spike
12. Swedish wire splicing spike
13. Screwdriver
14. Pliers
15. Small adjustable spanner
16. Knife
17. Can of 3 in 1 Oil (lubricating/penetrating oil)